Ben Forta

T0176313

Sams **Teach Yourself**

SQL

in **10 Minutes**

Fifth Edition

221 River Street, Hoboken, NJ 07030

Sams Teach Yourself SQL in 10 Minutes, Fifth Edition

ISBN-13: 978-0-13-518279-6

ISBN-10: 0-13-518279-4

Library of Congress Control Number: 2019910840

642 2024

Trademarks

All terms mentioned in this book that are known to be trademarks or service marks have been appropriately capitalized. Sams Publishing cannot attest to the accuracy of this information. Use of a term in this book should not be regarded as affecting the validity of any trademark or service mark.

Warning and Disclaimer

Every effort has been made to make this book as complete and as accurate as possible, but no warranty or fitness is implied. The information provided is on an "as is" basis. The author and the publisher shall have neither liability nor responsibility to any person or entity with respect to any loss or damages arising from the information contained in this book.

Special Sales

For information about buying this title in bulk quantities, or for special sales opportunities (which may include electronic versions; custom cover designs; and content particular to your business, training goals, marketing focus, or branding interests), please contact our corporate sales department at corpsales@pearsoned.com or (800) 382-3419.

For government sales inquiries, please contact governmentsales@pearsoned.com.

For questions about sales outside the U.S., please contact intlcs@pearson.com.

Cover credit mickyteam/Shutterstock

Editor-in-Chief
Mark Taub

Acquisitions Editor
Kim Spenceley

Development Editor
Mark Taber

Managing Editor
Sandra Schroeder

Project Editor
Mandie Frank

Copy Editor
Chuck Hutchinson

Indexer
Tim Wright

Proofreader
Abigail Manheim

Technical Editor
Benjamin Schupak

Designer
Chuti Prasertsith

Compositor
codeMantra

Contents at a Glance

Table of Contents

About the Author

Ben Forta is Adobe's Senior Director of Education Initiatives and has three decades of experience in the computer industry in product development, support, training, and product marketing. He is the author of the best-selling *Sams Teach Yourself SQL in 10 Minutes* (including spinoff titles on MariaDB, MySQL, SQL Server T-SQL, and Oracle PL/SQL), *Learning Regular Expressions*, as well as books on Java, Windows, and more. He has extensive experience in database design and development, has implemented databases for several highly successful commercial software programs and websites, and is a frequent lecturer and columnist on application development and Internet technologies. Ben lives in Oak Park, Michigan, with his wife, Marcy, and their children. He welcomes your email at ben@forta.com and invites you to visit his website at http://forta.com.

Acknowledgments

Thanks to the team at Sams for all these years of support, dedication, and encouragement. Over the past two decades, we've created 40+ books together, but this little volume is my favorite by far, and I thank you for giving me the creative freedom to evolve it as I see fit.

Thank you to Amazon.com reviewers who suggested the inclusion of the Challenges, which are new to this fifth edition.

Thanks to the many thousands of you who provided feedback on the first four editions of this book. Fortunately, most of it was positive, and all of it was appreciated. The enhancements and changes in this edition are a direct response to your feedback, which I continue to welcome.

Thanks to the dozens of colleges and universities that have made this book part of their IT and computer science curriculums. Being included and trusted by professors and teachers this way is immensely rewarding and equally humbling.

And finally, thanks to the almost half-million of you who bought the previous editions (and spinoffs) of this book, making it not just my best-selling title, but also the best-selling book on the subject. Your continued support is the highest compliment an author can ever be paid.

—Ben Forta

We Want to Hear from You!

As the reader of this book, *you* are our most important critic and commentator. We value your opinion and want to know what we're doing right, what we could do better, what areas you'd like to see us publish in, and any other words of wisdom you're willing to pass our way.

We welcome your comments. You can email or write to let us know what you did or didn't like about this book—as well as what we can do to make our books better.

Please note that we cannot help you with technical problems related to the topic of this book.

When you write, please be sure to include this book's title and author as well as your name and email address. We will carefully review your comments and share them with the author and editors who worked on the book.

Email: community@informit.com

Reader Services

Register your copy of *Sams Teach Yourself SQL in 10 Minutes a Day* at informit.com for convenient access to downloads, updates, and corrections as they become available. To start the registration process, go to informit.com/register and log in or create an account*. Enter the product ISBN, 9780135182796, and click Submit. Once the process is complete, you will find any available bonus content under Registered Products.

*Be sure to check the box that you would like to hear from us in order to receive exclusive discounts on future editions of this product.

Introduction

SQL is the most widely used database language. Whether you are an application developer, database administrator, web application designer, mobile app developer, or a user of popular data reporting tools, a good working knowledge of SQL is an important part of interacting with databases.

This book was born out of necessity. I had been teaching Web application development for several years, and students were constantly asking for SQL book recommendations. There are lots of SQL books out there. Some are actually very good. But they all have one thing in common: for most users they teach just too much information. Instead of teaching SQL itself, most books teach everything from database design and normalization to relational database theory and administrative concerns. And while those are all important topics, they are not of interest to most of us who just need to learn SQL.

And so, not finding a single book that I felt comfortable recommending, I turned that classroom experience into the book you are holding. *Sams Teach Yourself SQL in 10 Minutes* will teach you SQL you need to know, starting with simple data retrieval and working on to more complex topics including the use of joins, subqueries, stored procedures, cursors, triggers, and table constraints. You'll learn methodically, systematically, and simply—in lessons that will each take 10 minutes or less to complete.

Now in its fifth edition, this book has taught SQL to almost a half million English-speaking users, and has been translated into over a dozen other languages too so as to help users the world over.

New to this edition is the inclusion of lesson-specific challenges at the end of each lesson 2 - 18. They provide a chance for you to take the SQL you have learned and apply it to different scenarios and problems. The answers to each are not in the book, but, don't worry, you can find them on the book web page at http://forta.com/books/0135182794.

Now it is your turn. Turn to Lesson 1, and get to work. You'll be writing world-class SQL in no time at all.

Who Is the Teach Yourself SQL Book For?

This book is for you if

- ▶ You are new to SQL.
- ▶ You want to quickly learn how to get the most out of SQL.

▶ You want to learn how to use SQL in your own application development.

▶ You want to be productive quickly and easily in SQL without having to call someone for help.

DBMSs Covered in This Book

For the most part, the SQL taught in this book will apply to any Database Management System (DBMS). However, as all SQL implementations are not created equal, the following DBMSs are explicitly covered (and specific instructions or notes are included where needed):

▶ IBM DB2 (including DB2 in the cloud)

▶ Microsoft SQL Server (including Microsoft SQL Server Express)

▶ MariaDB

▶ MySQL

▶ Oracle (including Oracle Express)

▶ PostgreSQL

▶ SQLite

Example databases (or SQL scripts to create the example databases) are available for all of these DBMSs on the book web page at
`http://forta.com/books/0135182794`.

Conventions Used in This Book

This book uses different typefaces to differentiate between code and regular English, and also to help you identify important concepts.

Text that you type and text that should appear on your screen is presented in `monospace` type.

`It will look like this to mimic the way text looks on your screen.`

The text that makes up programming code has no color. But most tools used to create and edit code (in all programming languages, including SQL) do display code in color. The reason for doing so is that this makes it easier to read long code sequences, and it also helps spot typos and errors (when colors don't match or look right you know something is wrong). The SQL code throughout this book is printed in color with different colors used for SQL statements, clauses, strings, numbers, comments, and so on. Just be aware that there is no standard way to color code and different tools use different color schemes, so the colors you see in your own editor while trying the examples may not exactly match what's in the book.

This arrow (➥) at the beginning of a line of code means that a single line of code is too long to fit on the printed page. Continue typing all the characters after the ➥ as though they were part of the preceding line.

NOTE:

A Note presents interesting pieces of information related to the surrounding discussion.

TIP:

A Tip offers advice or teaches an easier way to do something.

CAUTION:

A Caution advises you about potential problems and helps you steer clear of disaster.

PLAIN ENGLISH:

New Term icons provide clear definitions of new, essential terms.

Input ▼

The Input icon identifies code that you can type in. It usually appears next to a listing.

Output ▼

The Output icon highlights the output produced by running a program. It usually appears after a listing.

Analysis ▼

The Analysis icon alerts you to the author's line-by-line analysis of a program.

Understanding SQL

In this lesson, you'll learn exactly what SQL is and what it will do for you.

Database Basics

The fact that you are reading a book on SQL indicates that you, somehow, need to interact with databases. SQL is a language used to do just this, so before looking at SQL itself, it is important that you understand some basic concepts about databases and database technologies.

Whether you are aware of it or not, you use databases all the time. Each time you select a contact on your phone or a name from your email address book, you are using a database. If you conduct a Google search, you are using a database. When you log in to your network at work, you are validating your name and password against a database. Even when you use your ATM card at a cash machine, you are using databases for PIN verification and balance checking.

But even though we all use databases all the time, there remains much confusion over what exactly a database is. This is especially true because different people use the same database terms to mean different things. Therefore, a good place to start our study is with a list and explanation of the most important database terms.

TIP: **Reviewing Basic Concepts**

What follows is a very brief overview of some basic database concepts. It is intended to either jolt your memory if you already have some database experience, or to provide you with the absolute basics if you are new to databases. Understanding databases is an important part of mastering SQL, and you might want to find a good book on database fundamentals to brush up on the subject if needed.

Databases

The term *database* is used in many different ways, but for our purposes (and indeed, from SQL's perspective) a database is a collection of data stored in some organized fashion. The simplest way to think of it is to imagine a database as a filing cabinet.

The filing cabinet is simply a physical location to store data, regardless of what that data is or how it is organized.

NEW TERM: **Database**
A container (usually a file or set of files) to store organized data.

CAUTION: **Misuse Causes Confusion**
People often use the term *database* to refer to the database software they are running. This is incorrect and a source of much confusion. Database software is actually called the *Database Management System* (or DBMS). The database is the container created and manipulated via the DBMS, and exactly what the database is and what form it takes vary from one database to the next.

Tables

When you store information in your filing cabinet, you don't just toss it in a drawer. Rather, you create files within the filing cabinet, and then you file related data in specific files.

In the database world, that file is called a table. A *table* is a structured file that can store data of a specific type. A table might contain a list of customers, a product catalog, or any other list of information.

NEW TERM: **Table**
A structured list of data of a specific type.

The key here is that the data stored in the table is one type of data or one list. You would never store a list of customers and a list of orders in the same database table. Doing so would make subsequent retrieval and access difficult. Rather, you'd create two tables, one for each list.

Every table in a database has a name that identifies it. That name is always unique—meaning no other table in that database can have the same name.

NOTE: **Table Names**
What makes a table name unique is actually a combination of several things including the database name and table name. Some databases also use the name of the database owner as part of the unique name. This means that while you cannot use the same table name twice in the same database, you definitely can reuse table names in different databases.

Tables have characteristics and properties that define how data is stored in them. These include information about what data may be stored, how it is broken up, how individual pieces of information are named, and much more. This set of information that describes a table is known as a *schema*, and schemas are used to describe specific tables within a database, as well as entire databases (and the relationship between tables in them, if any).

> NEW TERM: **Schema**
>
> Information about database and table layout and properties.

Columns and Datatypes

Tables are made up of columns. A *column* contains a particular piece of information within a table.

> NEW TERM: **Column**
>
> A single field in a table. All tables are made up of one or more columns.

The best way to understand this is to envision database tables as grids, somewhat like spreadsheets. Each column in the grid contains a particular piece of information. In a customer table, for example, one column contains the customer number, another contains the customer name, and the address, city, state, and ZIP code are all stored in their own columns.

> TIP: **Breaking Up Data**
>
> It is extremely important to break data into multiple columns correctly. For example, city, state, and ZIP (or postal) code should always be separate columns. When you break these out, it becomes possible to sort or filter data by specific columns (for example, to find all customers in a particular state or in a particular city). If city and state are combined into one column, it would be extremely difficult to sort or filter by state.
>
> When you break up data, the level of granularity is up to you and your specific requirements. For example, addresses are typically stored with the house number and street name together. This is fine, unless you might one day need to sort data by street name, in which case splitting house number and street name would be preferable.

Each column in a database has an associated datatype. A *datatype* defines what type of data the column can contain. For example, if the column were to contain a number (perhaps the number of items in an order), the datatype would be a numeric datatype.

If the column were to contain dates, text, notes, currency amounts, and so on, the appropriate datatype would be used to specify this.

NEW TERM: **Datatype**

A type of allowed data. Every table column has an associated datatype that restricts (or allows) specific data in that column.

Datatypes restrict the type of data that can be stored in a column (for example, preventing the entry of alphabetical characters into a numeric field). Datatypes also help sort data correctly and play an important role in optimizing disk usage. As such, special attention must be given to picking the right datatype when tables are created.

CAUTION: **Datatype Compatibility**

Datatypes and their names are one of the primary sources of SQL incompatibility. While most basic datatypes are supported consistently, many more advanced datatypes are not. And worse, occasionally you'll find that the same datatype is referred to by different names in different DBMSs. There is not much you can do about this, but it is important to keep in mind when you create table schemas.

Rows

Data in a table is stored in rows; each record saved is stored in its own *row*. Again, envisioning a table as a spreadsheet style grid, the vertical columns in the grid are the table columns, and the horizontal rows are the table rows.

For example, a customers table might store one customer per row. The number of rows in the table is the number of records in it.

NEW TERM: **Row**

A record in a table.

NOTE: **Records or Rows?**

You may hear users refer to database records when referring to rows. For the most part the two terms are used interchangeably, but row is technically the correct term.

Primary Keys

Every row in a table should have some column (or set of columns) that uniquely identifies it. A table containing customers might use a customer number column for this purpose, whereas a table containing orders might use the order ID. An employee list table might use an employee ID. A table containing a list of books might use the ISBN for this purpose.

> NEW TERM: **Primary key**
>
> A column (or set of columns) whose values uniquely identify every row in a table.

This column (or set of columns) that uniquely identifies each row in a table is called a *primary key*. The primary key is used to refer to a specific row. Without a primary key, updating or deleting specific rows in a table becomes extremely difficult as there is no guaranteed safe way to refer to just the rows to be affected.

> TIP: **Always Define Primary Keys**
>
> Although primary keys are not actually required, most database designers ensure that every table they create has a primary key so that future data manipulation is possible and manageable.

Any column in a table can be defined as the primary key, as long as it meets the following conditions:

- ▶ No two rows can have the same primary key value.
- ▶ Every row must have a value in the primary key column(s). (So, no NULL values.)
- ▶ Values in primary key columns should never be modified or updated.
- ▶ Primary key values should never be reused. (If a row is deleted from the table, its primary key may not be assigned to any new rows in the future.)

Primary keys are usually defined on a single column within a table. But this is not required, and multiple columns may be used together as a primary key. When multiple columns are used, the rules listed above must apply to all columns, and the values of all columns together must be unique (individual columns need not have unique values).

There is another very important type of key called a foreign key, but I'll get to that later on in Lesson 12, "Joining Tables."

What Is SQL?

SQL (pronounced as the letters S-Q-L or as *sequel*) is an abbreviation for Structured Query Language. SQL is a language designed specifically for communicating with databases.

Unlike other languages (spoken languages like English, or programming languages like Java, C, or Python), SQL is made up of very few words. This is deliberate. SQL is designed to do one thing and do it well—provide you with a simple and efficient way to read and write data from a database.

What are the advantages of SQL?

▶ SQL is not a proprietary language used by specific database vendors. Almost every major DBMS supports SQL, so learning this one language will enable you to interact with just about every database you'll run into.

▶ SQL is easy to learn. The statements are all made up of descriptive English words, and there aren't that many of them.

▶ Despite its apparent simplicity, SQL is a very powerful language, and by cleverly using and combining its language elements, you can perform very complex and sophisticated database operations.

And with that, let's learn SQL.

NOTE: **SQL Extensions**

Many DBMS vendors have extended their support for SQL by adding statements or instructions to the language. The purpose of these extensions is to provide additional functionality or simplified ways to perform specific operations. And while often extremely useful, these extensions tend to be very DBMS specific, and they are rarely supported by more than a single vendor.

Standard SQL is governed by the ANSI standards committee, and is thus called ANSI SQL. All major DBMSs, even those with their own extensions, support ANSI SQL. Individual implementations have their own names (PL-SQL, used by Oracle; Transact-SQL, used by Microsoft SQL Server; and so on).

For the most part, the SQL taught in this book is ANSI SQL. On the odd occasion where DBMS-specific SQL is used, it is so noted.

Try It Yourself

As with any language, the best way to learn SQL is to try it for yourself. To do this, you'll need a database and an application with which to test your SQL statements.

All of the lessons in this book use real SQL statements and real database tables, and you should have access to a DBMS to follow along.

> TIP: **Which DBMS Should You Use?**
>
> You need access to a DBMS to follow along. But which should you use?
>
> The good news is that the SQL you'll learn in this book is relevant to every major DBMS. As such, your choice of DBMS should primarily be based on convenience and simplicity.
>
> There are basically two ways to proceed. You can install a DBMS (and supporting client software) on your own computer; this will give you the greatest access and control. But for many, the trickiest part of getting started learning SQL is actually getting a DBMS installed and configured. The alternative is to access a remote (or cloud-based) DBMS; this way you have nothing to manage and install.
>
> You have lots of options if you decide to install your own DBMS. Here are a couple of suggestions:
>
> ▶ MySQL (or its spin-off MariaDB) is a really good choice in that it is free, supported on every major operating system, is easy to install, and is one of the most popular DBMSs in use. MySQL comes with a command-line tool for actually entering your SQL, but you are better using the optional MySQL Workbench, so download that, too (it's usually a separate install).
>
> ▶ Windows users may want to use Microsoft SQL Server Express. This free version of the popular and powerful SQL Server includes a user-friendly client named SQL Server Management Studio.
>
> The alternative is to use a remote (or cloud-based) DBMS:
>
> ▶ If you are learning SQL to use at work, your employer may have a DBMS that you can use. If this is an option, you'll likely be given your own DBMS login and a tool to use to connect to the DBMS to enter and test your SQL.
>
> ▶ Cloud-based DBMSs are instances of DBMSs running on virtual servers, effectively giving you the benefits of your own DBMS without having to actually install one locally. All of the major cloud service vendors (including Google, Amazon, and Microsoft) offer DBMSs in the cloud. Unfortunately, at the time of this book's writing, setting these up (including configuring secure remote access) isn't trivial and is often more work than installing your own DBMS locally. The exceptions are Oracle's Live SQL and IBM's Db2 on Cloud, which offer a free version that includes a web interface. Just type your SQL in the web browser, and you're good to go.
>
> You'll find links to all the options mentioned here on the book's web page, and as DBMS options evolve that page will be updated with tips and suggestions.

Once you have access to a DBMS, Appendix A, "Sample Table Scripts," explains what the example tables are and provides details on how to obtain (or create) them so that can may follow along with the instructions in each lesson.

In addition, starting in Lesson 2 you'll find Challenges after the "Summary" section. They present you with the opportunity to take your newly acquired SQL knowledge and apply it to solve problems not explicitly mentioned in the lessons. To verify your solutions (or if you get stuck and need some help), visit the book's web page.

Summary

In this first lesson, you learned what SQL is and why it is useful. Because SQL is used to interact with databases, you also reviewed some basic database terminology.

LESSON 2

Retrieving Data

In this lesson, you'll learn how to use the all-important SELECT *statement to retrieve one or more columns of data from a table.*

The SELECT Statement

As explained in Lesson 1, "Understanding SQL," SQL statements are made up of plain English terms. These terms are called keywords, and every SQL statement is made up of one or more keywords. The SQL statement that you'll probably use most frequently is the SELECT statement. Its purpose is to retrieve information from one or more tables.

> **NEW TERM: Keyword**
> A reserved word that is part of the SQL language. Never name a table or column using a keyword. Appendix D, "SQL Reserved Words," lists some of the more common reserved words.

To use SELECT to retrieve table data, you must, at a minimum, specify two pieces of information—what you want to select and from where you want to select it.

> **NOTE: Following Along with the Examples**
> The sample SQL statements (and sample output) throughout the lessons in this book use a set of data files that are described in Appendix A, "Sample Table Scripts." If you'd like to follow along and try the examples yourself (I strongly recommend that you do so), refer to Appendix A, which contains instructions on how to download or create these data files.

> **TIP: Use the Right Database**
> DBMSs allow you to work with multiple databases (the filing cabinet in the analogy in Lesson 1). When you installed the sample tables (as per Appendix A), you were advised to install them in a new database. If you did so, make sure you select that database before proceeding, just as you did when you created and populated the sample tables. As you work through these lessons, if you encounter errors about unknown tables, then you most likely are in the wrong database.

Retrieving Individual Columns

We'll start with a simple SQL SELECT statement, as follows:

Input ▼

```
SELECT prod_name
FROM Products;
```

Analysis ▼

The previous statement uses the SELECT statement to retrieve a single column called prod_name from the Products table. The desired column name is specified right after the SELECT keyword, and the FROM keyword specifies the name of the table from which to retrieve the data. The output from this statement is shown in the following:

Output ▼

```
prod_name
--------------------
Fish bean bag toy
Bird bean bag toy
Rabbit bean bag toy
8 inch teddy bear
12 inch teddy bear
18 inch teddy bear
Raggedy Ann
King doll
Queen doll
```

Depending on the DBMS and client you are using, you may also see a message telling you how many rows were retrieved and the processing time. For example, the MySQL command line would display something like this:

```
9 rows in set (0.01 sec)
```

> NOTE: **Unsorted Data**
> If you tried this query yourself, you might have discovered that the data was displayed in a different order than shown here. If this is the case, don't worry—it is working exactly as it is supposed to. If query results are not explicitly sorted (we'll get to that in the next lesson), then data will be returned in no order of any significance. It may be the order in which the data was added to the table, but it may not. As long as your query returned the same number of rows, then it is working.

A simple SELECT statement similar to the one used above returns all the rows in a table. Data is not filtered (so as to retrieve a subset of the results), nor is it sorted. We'll discuss these topics in the next few lessons.

> TIP: **Terminating Statements**
>
> Multiple SQL statements must be separated by semicolons (the ; character). Most DBMSs do not require that a semicolon be specified after single statements. But if your particular DBMS complains, you might have to add it there. Of course, you can always add a semicolon if you wish. It'll do no harm, even if it is, in fact, not needed.

> NOTE: **SQL Statement and Case**
>
> It is important to note that SQL statements are *not* case sensitive, so SELECT is the same as select, which is the same as Select. Many SQL developers find that using uppercase for all SQL keywords and lowercase for column and table names makes code easier to read and debug. However, be aware that while the SQL language is case-insensitive, the names of tables, columns, and values may not be (that depends on your DBMS and how it is configured).

> TIP: **Use of White Space**
>
> All extra white space within a SQL statement is ignored when that statement is processed. SQL statements can be specified on one long line or broken up over many lines. So, the following three statements are functionally identical:

```
SELECT prod_name
FROM Products;

SELECT prod_name FROM Products;

SELECT
prod_name
FROM
Products;
```

> Most SQL developers find that breaking up statements over multiple lines makes them easier to read and debug.

Retrieving Multiple Columns

To retrieve multiple columns from a table, the same SELECT statement is used. The only difference is that multiple column names must be specified after the SELECT keyword, and each column must be separated by a comma.

TIP: **Take Care with Commas**

When selecting multiple columns, be sure to specify a comma between each column name, but not after the last column name. Doing so will generate an error.

The following SELECT statement retrieves three columns from the Products table:

Input ▼

```
SELECT prod_id, prod_name, prod_price
FROM Products;
```

Analysis ▼

Just as in the prior example, this statement uses the SELECT statement to retrieve data from the Products table. In this example, three column names are specified, each separated by a comma. The output from this statement is shown below:

Output ▼

```
prod_id     prod_name              prod_price
--------    --------------------   ----------
BNBG01      Fish bean bag toy            3.49
BNBG02      Bird bean bag toy            3.49
BNBG03      Rabbit bean bag toy          3.49
BR01        8 inch teddy bear            5.99
BR02        12 inch teddy bear           8.99
BR03        18 inch teddy bear          11.99
RGAN01      Raggedy Ann                  4.99
RYL01       King doll                    9.49
RYL02       Queen dool                   9.49
```

NOTE: **Presentation of Data**

SQL statements typically return raw, unformatted data, and different DBMSs and clients may display the data differently (with different alignment or decimal places, for example). Data formatting is a presentation issue, not a retrieval issue. Therefore, presentation is typically specified in the application that displays the data. Actual retrieved data (without application-provided formatting) is rarely used.

Retrieving All Columns

In addition to being able to specify desired columns (one or more, as seen above), SELECT statements can also request all columns without having to list them individually. This is done using the asterisk (*) wildcard character in lieu of actual column names, as follows:

Input ▼

```
SELECT *
FROM Products;
```

Analysis ▼

When a wildcard (*) is specified, all the columns in the table are returned. The column order will typically, but not always, be the physical order in which the columns appear in the table definition. However, SQL data is seldom displayed as is. (Usually, it is returned to an application that formats or presents the data as needed). As such, this should not pose a problem.

> CAUTION: **Using Wildcards**
>
> As a rule, you are better off not using the * wildcard unless you really do need every column in the table. Even though use of wildcards may save you the time and effort needed to list the desired columns explicitly, retrieving unnecessary columns usually slows down the performance of your retrieval and your application.

> TIP: **Retrieving Unknown Columns**
>
> There is one big advantage to using wildcards. As you do not explicitly specify column names (because the asterisk retrieves every column), it is possible to retrieve columns whose names are unknown.

Retrieving Distinct Rows

As you have seen, SELECT returns all matched rows. But what if you do not want every occurrence of every value? For example, suppose you want the vendor ID of all vendors with products in your Products table:

Input ▼

```
SELECT vend_id
FROM Products;
```

Output ▼

```
vend_id
----------
BRS01
BRS01
BRS01
DLL01
DLL01
DLL01
DLL01
FNG01
FNG01
```

The SELECT statement returned nine rows (even though there are only three unique vendors in that list) because there are nine products listed in the Products table. So how could you retrieve a list of distinct values?

The solution is to use the DISTINCT keyword, which, as its name implies, instructs the database to only return distinct values.

Input ▼

```
SELECT DISTINCT vend_id
FROM Products;
```

Analysis ▼

SELECT DISTINCT vend_id tells the DBMS to only return distinct (unique) vend_id rows, and so only three rows are returned, as seen in the following output. If used, the DISTINCT keyword must be placed directly in front of the column names.

Output ▼

```
vend_id
----------
BRS01
DLL01
FNG01
```

> CAUTION: **Can't Be Partially DISTINCT**
>
> The DISTINCT keyword applies to all columns, not just the one it precedes. If you were to specify SELECT DISTINCT vend_id, prod_price, six of the nine rows would be retrieved because the combined specified columns produced six unique combinations. To see the difference, try these two statements and compare the results:
>
> SELECT DISTINCT vend_id, prod_price FROM Products;
> SELECT vend_id, prod_price FROM Products;

Limiting Results

SELECT statements return all matched rows, possibly every row in the specified table. What if you want to return just the first row or a set number of rows? This is doable, but unfortunately, this is one of those situations where all SQL implementations are not created equal.

In Microsoft SQL Server you can use the TOP keyword to limit the top number of entries, as seen here:

Input ▼

```
SELECT TOP 5 prod_name
FROM Products;
```

Output ▼

```
prod_name
-----------------
8 inch teddy bear
12 inch teddy bear
18 inch teddy bear
Fish bean bag toy
Bird bean bag toy
```

Analysis ▼

The previous statement uses the SELECT TOP 5 statement to retrieve just the first five rows.

If you are using DB2, well, then you get to use SQL unique to that DBMS, like this:

Input ▼

```
SELECT prod_name
FROM Products
FETCH FIRST 5 ROWS ONLY;
```

Analysis ▼

FETCH FIRST 5 ROWS ONLY does exactly what it suggests.

If you are using Oracle, you need to count rows based on ROWNUM (a row number counter) like this:

Input ▼

```
SELECT prod_name
FROM Products
WHERE ROWNUM <=5;
```

If you are using MySQL, MariaDB, PostgreSQL, or SQLite, you can use the LIMIT clause, as follows:

Input ▼

```
SELECT prod_name
FROM Products
LIMIT 5;
```

Analysis ▼

The previous statement uses the SELECT statement to retrieve a single column. LIMIT 5 instructs the supported DBMSs to return no more than five rows. The output from this statement is shown in the following code.

To get the next five rows, specify both where to start and the number of rows to retrieve, like this:

Input ▼

```
SELECT prod_name
FROM Products
LIMIT 5 OFFSET 5;
```

Analysis ▼

LIMIT 5 OFFSET 5 instructs supported DBMSs to return five rows starting from row 5. The first number is the number of rows to retrieve, and the second is where to start. The output from this statement is shown in the following code:

Output ▼

```
prod_name
-------------------
Rabbit bean bag toy
Raggedy Ann
King doll
Queen doll
```

So, LIMIT specifies the number of rows to return. LIMIT with an OFFSET specifies where to start from. In our example, there are only nine products in the Products table, so LIMIT 5 OFFSET 5 returned just four rows (as there was no fifth).

> CAUTION: **Row 0**
> The first row retrieved is row 0, not row 1. As such, LIMIT 1 OFFSET 1 will retrieve the second row, not the first one.

> TIP: **MySQL, MariaDB, and SQLite Shortcut**
>
> MySQL, MariaDB, and SQLite support a shorthand version of LIMIT 4
> OFFSET 3, enabling you to combine them as LIMIT 3,4. Using this syntax,
> the value before the , is the OFFSET and the value after the , is the LIMIT
> (yes, they are reversed, so be careful).

> NOTE: **Not ALL SQL Is Created Equal**
>
> I included this section on limiting results for one reason only—to demonstrate
> that while SQL is usually quite consistent across implementations, you can't
> rely on it always being so. While very basic statements tend to be very portable,
> more complex ones tend to be less so. Keep that in mind as you search for
> SQL solutions to specific problems.

Using Comments

As you have seen, SQL statements are instructions that are processed by your DBMS.
But what if you wanted to include text that you'd not want processed and executed?
Why would you ever want to do this? Here are a few reasons:

► The SQL statements we've been using here are all very short and very
  simple. But, as your SQL statements grow (in length and complexity),
  you'll want to include descriptive comments (for your own future reference
  or for whoever has to work on the project next). These comments need to
  be embedded in the SQL scripts, but they are obviously not intended for
  actual DBMS processing. (For an example of this, see the create.sql and
  populate.sql files used in Appendix B, "SQL Statement Syntax").

► The same is true for headers at the top of a SQL file (one that is saving
  SQL statements perhaps for future use), usually containing a description and
  notes, and perhaps even programmer contact information. (This use case is
  also seen in the Appendix B .sql files.).

► Another important use for comments is to temporarily stop SQL code from
  being executed. If you were working with a long SQL statement, and wanted
  to test just part of it, you could *comment out* some of the code so that DBMS
  sees it as comments and ignores it.

Most DBMSs support several forms of comment syntax. We'll start with inline comments:

Input ▼

```
SELECT prod_name    -- this is a comment
FROM Products;
```

Analysis ▼

Comments may be embedded inline using -- (two hyphens). Any text on the same line that is after the -- is considered comment text, making this a good option for describing columns in a CREATE TABLE statement, for example.

Here is another form of inline comment (although less commonly supported):

Input ▼

```
# This is a comment
SELECT prod_name
FROM Products;
```

Analysis ▼

A # at the start of a line makes the entire line a comment. You can see this format comment used in the accompanying create.sql and populate.sql scripts.

You can also create multiline comments and comments that stop and start anywhere within the script:

Input ▼

```
/* SELECT prod_name, vend_id
FROM Products; */
SELECT prod_name
FROM Products;
```

Analysis ▼

/* starts a comment, and */ ends it. Anything between /* and */ is comment text. This type of comment is often used to *comment out* code, as seen in this example. Here, two SELECT statements are defined, but the first won't execute because it has been commented out.

Summary

In this lesson, you learned how to use the SQL SELECT statement to retrieve a single table column, multiple table columns, and all table columns. You also learned how to return distinct values and how to comment your code. And unfortunately, you were also introduced to the fact that more complex SQL tends to be less portable SQL. Next, you'll learn how to sort the retrieved data.

Challenges

1. Write a SQL statement to retrieve all customer IDs (`cust_id`) from the `Customers` table.

2. The `OrderItems` table contains every item ordered (and some were ordered multiple times). Write a SQL statement to retrieve a list of the products (`prod_id`) ordered (not every order, just a unique list of products). Here's a hint: you should end up with seven unique rows displayed.

3. Write a SQL statement that retrieves all columns from the `Customers` table and an alternate `SELECT` that retrieves just the customer ID. Use comments to comment out one `SELECT` so as to be able to run the other. (And, of course, test both statements.)

TIP: **Where Are the Answers?**

Challenge answers are on the book's web page:
`http://forta.com/books/0135182794`.

LESSON 3

Sorting Retrieved Data

In this lesson, you will learn how to use the SELECT *statement's* ORDER BY *clause to sort retrieved data as needed.*

Sorting Data

As you learned in the last lesson, the following SQL statement returns a single column from a database table. But look at the output. The data appears to be displayed in no particular order at all.

Input ▼

```
SELECT prod_name
FROM Products;
```

Output ▼

```
prod_name
--------------------
Fish bean bag toy
Bird bean bag toy
Rabbit bean bag toy
8 inch teddy bear
12 inch teddy bear
18 inch teddy bear
Raggedy Ann
King doll
Queen doll
```

Actually, the retrieved data is not displayed in a mere random order. If unsorted, data will typically be displayed in the order in which it appears in the underlying tables. This could be the order in which the data was added to the tables initially. However, if data was subsequently updated or deleted, the order will be affected by how the DBMS reuses reclaimed storage space. The end result is that you cannot (and should not) rely on the sort order if you do not explicitly control it. Relational database

design theory states that the sequence of retrieved data cannot be assumed to have
significance if ordering was not explicitly specified.

NEW TERM: **Clause**

SQL statements are made up of clauses, some required and some optional.
A clause usually consists of a keyword and supplied data. An example of this is
the SELECT statement's FROM clause, which you saw in the last lesson.

To explicitly sort data retrieved using a SELECT statement, you use the ORDER BY
clause. ORDER BY takes the name of one or more columns by which to sort the output.
Look at the following example:

Input ▼

```
SELECT prod_name
FROM Products
ORDER BY prod_name;
```

Analysis ▼

This statement is identical to the earlier statement, except it also specifies an ORDER BY
clause instructing the DBMS software to sort the data by the prod_name column. The
results are as follows:

Output ▼

```
prod_name
--------------------
12 inch teddy bear
18 inch teddy bear
8 inch teddy bear
Bird bean bag toy
Fish bean bag toy
King doll
Queen doll
Rabbit bean bag toy
Raggedy Ann
```

CAUTION: **Position of** ORDER BY **Clause**

When specifying an ORDER BY clause, be sure that it is the last clause in your
SELECT statement. If it is not the last clause, an error will be generated.

> TIP: **Sorting by Nonselected Columns**
>
> Although more often than not the columns used in an ORDER BY clause will be ones selected for display, this is actually not required. It is perfectly legal to sort data by a column that is not retrieved.

Sorting by Multiple Columns

It is often necessary to sort data by more than one column. For example, if you are displaying an employee list, you might want to display it sorted by last name and first name (first by last name, and then within each last name sort by first name). This type of sort would be useful if there are multiple employees with the same last name.

To sort by multiple columns, simply specify the column names separated by commas (just as you do when you are selecting multiple columns).

The following code retrieves three columns and sorts the results by two of them—first by price and then by name.

Input ▼

```
SELECT prod_id, prod_price, prod_name
FROM Products
ORDER BY prod_price, prod_name;
```

Output ▼

```
prod_id    prod_price    prod_name
-------    ----------    --------------------
BNBG02     3.4900        Bird bean bag toy
BNBG01     3.4900        Fish bean bag toy
BNBG03     3.4900        Rabbit bean bag toy
RGAN01     4.9900        Raggedy Ann
BR01       5.9900        8 inch teddy bear
BR02       8.9900        12 inch teddy bear
RYL01      9.4900        King doll
RYL02      9.4900        Queen doll
BR03       11.9900       18 inch teddy bear
```

It is important to understand that when you are sorting by multiple columns, the sort sequence is exactly as specified. In other words, using the output in the example above, the products are sorted by the prod_name column only when multiple rows have the same prod_price value. If all the values in the prod_price column had been unique, no data would have been sorted by prod_name.

Sorting by Column Position

In addition to being able to specify sort order using column names, ORDER BY also supports ordering specified by relative column position. The best way to understand this is to look at an example:

Input ▼

```
SELECT prod_id, prod_price, prod_name
FROM Products
ORDER BY 2, 3;
```

Output ▼

```
prod_id    prod_price    prod_name
-------    ----------    --------------------
BNBG02     3.4900        Bird bean bag toy
BNBG01     3.4900        Fish bean bag toy
BNBG03     3.4900        Rabbit bean bag toy
RGAN01     4.9900        Raggedy Ann
BR01       5.9900        8 inch teddy bear
BR02       8.9900        12 inch teddy bear
RYL01      9.4900        King doll
RYL02      9.4900        Queen doll
BR03       11.9900       18 inch teddy bear
```

Analysis ▼

As you can see, the output is identical to that of the query above. The difference here is in the ORDER BY clause. Instead of specifying column names, you specify the relative positions of selected columns in the SELECT list. ORDER BY 2 means sort by the second column in the SELECT list, the prod_price column. ORDER BY 2, 3 means sort by prod_price and then by prod_name.

The primary advantage of this technique is that it saves retyping the column names. But there are some downsides too. First, not explicitly listing column names increases the likelihood of you mistakenly specifying the wrong column. Second, it is all too easy to mistakenly reorder data when making changes to the SELECT list (forgetting to make the corresponding changes to the ORDER BY clause). And finally, obviously you cannot use this technique when sorting by columns that are not in the SELECT list.

> TIP: **Sorting by Nonselected Columns**
> This technique cannot be used when sorting by columns that do not appear in the SELECT list. However, you can mix and match actual column names and relative column positions in a single statement if needed.

Specifying Sort Direction

Data sorting is not limited to ascending sort orders (from A to Z). Although this is the default sort order, the ORDER BY clause can also be used to sort in descending order (from Z to A). To sort by descending order, you must specify the keyword DESC.

The following example sorts the products by price in descending order (most expensive first):

Input ▼

```
SELECT prod_id, prod_price, prod_name
FROM Products
ORDER BY prod_price DESC;
```

Output ▼

prod_id	prod_price	prod_name
BR03	11.9900	18 inch teddy bear
RYL01	9.4900	King doll
RYL02	9.4900	Queen doll
BR02	8.9900	12 inch teddy bear
BR01	5.9900	8 inch teddy bear
RGAN01	4.9900	Raggedy Ann
BNBG01	3.4900	Fish bean bag toy
BNBG02	3.4900	Bird bean bag toy
BNBG03	3.4900	Rabbit bean bag toy

But what if you were to sort by multiple columns? The following example sorts the products in descending order (most expensive first), plus product name:

Input ▼

```
SELECT prod_id, prod_price, prod_name
FROM Products
ORDER BY prod_price DESC, prod_name;
```

Output ▼

prod_id	prod_price	prod_name
BR03	11.9900	18 inch teddy bear
RYL01	9.4900	King doll
RYL02	9.4900	Queen doll
BR02	8.9900	12 inch teddy bear
BR01	5.9900	8 inch teddy bear
RGAN01	4.9900	Raggedy Ann
BNBG02	3.4900	Bird bean bag toy
BNBG01	3.4900	Fish bean bag toy
BNBG03	3.4900	Rabbit bean bag toy

Analysis ▼

The DESC keyword only applies to the column name that directly precedes it. In the example above, DESC was specified for the prod_price column, but not for the prod_name column. Therefore, the prod_price column is sorted in descending order, but the prod_name column (within each price) is still sorted in standard ascending order.

> CAUTION: **Sorting Descending on Multiple Columns**
>
> If you want to sort descending on multiple columns, be sure each column has its own DESC keyword.

It is worth noting that DESC is short for DESCENDING, and both keywords may be used. The opposite of DESC is ASC (or ASCENDING), which may be specified to sort in ascending order. In practice, however, ASC is not usually used because ascending order is the default sequence (and is assumed if neither ASC nor DESC is specified).

> TIP: **Case Sensitivity and Sort Orders**
>
> When you are sorting textual data, is A the same as a? And does a come before B or after z? These are not theoretical questions, and the answers depend on how the database is set up.
>
> In *dictionary* sort order, A is treated the same as a, and that is the default behavior for most DBMSs. However, most good DBMSs enable database administrators to change this behavior if needed. (If your database contains lots of foreign language characters, this might become necessary.)
>
> The key here is that, if you do need an alternate sort order, you may not be able to accomplish this with a simple ORDER BY clause. You may need to contact your database administrator.

Summary

In this lesson, you learned how to sort retrieved data using the SELECT statement's ORDER BY clause. This clause, which must be the last in the SELECT statement, can be used to sort data on one or more columns as needed.

Challenges

1. Write a SQL statement to retrieve all customer names (cust_names) from the Customers table, and display the results sorted from z to A.

2. Write a SQL statement to retrieve customer ID (cust_id) and order number (order_num) from the Orders table, and sort the results first by customer ID and then by order date in reverse chronological order.

3. Our fictitious store obviously prefers to sell more expensive items, and lots of them. Write a SQL statement to display the quantity and price (item_price) from the OrderItems table, sorted with the highest quantity and highest price first.

4. What is wrong with the following SQL statement? (Try to figure it out without running it):

```
SELECT vend_name,
FROM Vendors
ORDER vend_name DESC;
```

LESSON 4

Filtering Data

In this lesson, you will learn how to use the SELECT *statement's* WHERE *clause to specify search conditions.*

Using the WHERE Clause

Database tables usually contain large amounts of data, and you seldom need to retrieve all the rows in a table. More often than not you'll want to extract a subset of the table's data as needed for specific operations or reports. Retrieving just the data you want involves specifying *search criteria*, also known as a *filter condition*.

Within a SELECT statement, data is filtered by specifying search criteria in the WHERE clause. The WHERE clause is specified right after the table name (the FROM clause) as follows:

Input ▼

```
SELECT prod_name, prod_price
FROM Products
WHERE prod_price = 3.49;
```

Analysis ▼

This statement retrieves two columns from the products table, but instead of returning all rows, only rows with a prod_price value of 3.49 are returned, as follows:

Output ▼

```
prod_name              prod_price
-----------------      ----------
Fish bean bag toy      3.49
Bird bean bag toy      3.49
Rabbit bean bag toy    3.49
```

This example uses a simple equality test: It checks to see if a column has a specified value, and it filters the data accordingly. But SQL lets you do more than just test for equality.

TIP: **How Many Zeros?**

As you try the examples in this lesson, you may see results displayed as 3.49, 3.490, 3.4900, and so on. This behavior tends to be somewhat DBMS specific, as it is tied to the datatypes used and their default behavior. So, if your output is a little different from mine, don't sweat it; after all, 3.49 and 3.4900 are mathematically identical anyway.

TIP: **SQL Versus Application Filtering**

Data can also be filtered at the client application level, not in the DBMS but by whatever tool or application retrieves the data from the DBMS. To do this, the SQL SELECT statement retrieves more data than is actually required for the client application, and the client code loops through the returned data to extract just the needed rows.

As a rule, this practice is strongly discouraged. Databases are optimized to perform filtering quickly and efficiently. Making the client application (or development language) do the database's job will dramatically impact application performance and will create applications that cannot scale properly. In addition, if data is filtered at the client, the server has to send unneeded data across the network connections, resulting in a waste of network bandwidth usage.

CAUTION: WHERE **Clause Position**

When using both ORDER BY and WHERE clauses, make sure that ORDER BY comes after the WHERE. Otherwise, an error will be generated. (See Lesson 3, "Sorting Retrieved Data," for more information on using ORDER BY.)

The WHERE Clause Operators

The first WHERE clause we looked at tests for equality—determining if a column contains a specific value. SQL supports a whole range of conditional operators as listed in Table 4.1.

TABLE 4.1 WHERE Clause Operators

Operator	Description
=	Equality
<>	Nonequality
!=	Nonequality
<	Less than
<=	Less than or equal to
!<	Not less than
>	Greater than
>=	Greater than or equal to
!>	Not greater than
BETWEEN	Between two specified values
IS NULL	Is a NULL value

CAUTION: **Operator Compatibility**

Some of the operators listed in Table 4.1 are redundant; for example, <> is the same as !=. !< (not less than) accomplishes the same effect as >= (greater than or equal to). Not all of these operators are supported by all DBMSs. Refer to your DBMS documentation to determine exactly what it supports.

Checking Against a Single Value

We have already seen an example of testing for equality. Let's take a look at a few examples to demonstrate the use of other operators.

This first example lists all products that cost less than $10:

Input ▼

```
SELECT prod_name, prod_price
FROM Products
WHERE prod_price < 10;
```

Output ▼

```
prod_name              prod_price
-------------------    ----------
Fish bean bag toy      3.49
Bird bean bag toy      3.49
Rabbit bean bag toy    3.49
8 inch teddy bear      5.99
12 inch teddy bear     8.99
Raggedy Ann            4.99
King doll              9.49
Queen doll             9.49
```

This next statement retrieves all products costing $10 or less (although the result will be the same as in the previous example because there are no items with a price of exactly $10):

Input ▼

```
SELECT prod_name, prod_price
FROM Products
WHERE prod_price <= 10;
```

Checking for Nonmatches

This next example lists all products not made by vendor DLL01:

Input ▼

```
SELECT vend_id, prod_name
FROM Products
WHERE vend_id <> 'DLL01';
```

Output ▼

```
vend_id        prod_name
----------     ------------------
BRS01          8 inch teddy bear
BRS01          12 inch teddy bear
BRS01          18 inch teddy bear
FNG01          King doll
FNG01          Queen doll
```

> TIP: **When to Use Quotes**
> If you look closely at the conditions used in the above WHERE clauses, you will
> notice that some values are enclosed within single quotes, and others are not.
> The single quotes are used to delimit a string. If you are comparing a value
> against a column that is a string datatype, the delimiting quotes are required.
> Quotes are not used to delimit values used with numeric columns.

The following is the same example, except that this one uses the != operator instead
of <>:

Input ▼

```
SELECT vend_id, prod_name
FROM Products
WHERE vend_id != 'DLL01';
```

> CAUTION: != **or** <>?
> Usually, you can use != and <> interchangeably. However, not all DBMSs
> support both forms of the nonequality operator. If in doubt, consult your DBMS
> documentation.

Checking for a Range of Values

To check for a range of values, you can use the BETWEEN operator. Its syntax is a
little different from other WHERE clause operators because it requires two values: the
beginning and end of the range. The BETWEEN operator can be used, for example, to
check for all products that cost between $5 and $10 or for all dates that fall between
specified start and end dates.

The following example demonstrates the use of the BETWEEN operator by retrieving all
products with a price between $5 and $10:

Input ▼

```
SELECT prod_name, prod_price
FROM Products
WHERE prod_price BETWEEN 5 AND 10;
```

Output ▼

```
prod_name              prod_price
------------------     ----------
8 inch teddy bear         5.99
12 inch teddy bear        8.99
King doll                 9.49
Queen doll                9.49
```

Analysis ▼

As seen in this example, when BETWEEN is used, two values must be specified—the low end and high end of the desired range. The two values must also be separated by the AND keyword. BETWEEN matches all the values in the range, including the specified start and end values.

Checking for No Value

When a table is created, the table designer can specify whether or not individual columns can contain no value. When a column contains no value, it is said to contain a NULL value.

> NEW TERM: **NULL**
> *No value*, as opposed to a field containing 0, or an empty string, or just spaces.

To determine if a value is NULL, you cannot simply check to see if = NULL. Instead, the SELECT statement has a special WHERE clause that you can use to check for columns with NULL values—the IS NULL clause. The syntax looks like this:

Input ▼

```
SELECT prod_name
FROM Products
WHERE prod_price IS NULL;
```

This statement returns a list of all products that have no price (an empty prod_price field, not a price of 0), and because there are none, no data is returned. The Customers table, however, does contain columns with NULL values—the cust_email column will contain NULL if a customer has no email address on file:

Input ▼

```
SELECT cust_name
FROM Customers
WHERE cust_email IS NULL;
```

Output ▼

```
cust_name
----------
Kids Place
The Toy Store
```

> TIP: **DBMS-Specific Operators**
>
> Many DBMSs extend the standard set of operators, providing advanced filtering options. Refer to your DBMS documentation for more information.

> CAUTION: **NULL and Nonmatches**
>
> You might expect that when you filter to select all rows that do not have a particular value, rows with a NULL will be returned. But they will not. NULL is strange this way, and rows with NULL in the filter column are not returned when filtering for matches or when filtering for nonmatches.

Summary

In this lesson, you learned how to filter returned data using the SELECT statement's WHERE clause. You learned how to test for equality, nonequality, greater than and less than, and value ranges, as well as for NULL values.

Challenges

1. Write a SQL statement to retrieve the product ID (`prod_id`) and name (`prod_name`) from the `Products` table, returning only products with a price of `9.49`.

2. Write a SQL statement to retrieve the product ID (`prod_id`) and name (`prod_name`) from the `Products` table, returning only products with a price of `9` or more.

3. Now let's combine Lessons 3 and 4. Write a SQL statement that retrieves the unique list of order numbers (`order_num`) from the `OrderItems` table, which contain 100 or more of any item.

4. One more. Write a SQL statement that returns the product name (`prod_name`) and price (`prod_price`) from `Products` for all products priced between `3` and `6`. Oh, and sort the results by price. (There are multiple solutions to this one, and we'll revisit it in the next lesson, but you can solve it using what you've learned thus far.)

LESSON 5

Advanced Data Filtering

In this lesson, you'll learn how to combine WHERE clauses to create powerful and sophisticated search conditions. You'll also learn how to use the NOT and IN operators.

Combining WHERE Clauses

All the WHERE clauses introduced in Lesson 4, "Filtering Data," filter data using a single criterion. For a greater degree of filter control, SQL lets you specify multiple WHERE clauses. These clauses may be used in two ways: as AND clauses or as OR clauses.

> NEW TERM: **Operator**
> A special keyword used to join or change clauses within a WHERE clause. Also known as logical operators.

Using the AND Operator

To filter by more than one column, you use the AND operator to append conditions to your WHERE clause. The following code demonstrates this:

Input ▼

```
SELECT prod_id, prod_price, prod_name
FROM Products
WHERE vend_id = 'DLL01' AND prod_price <= 4;
```

Analysis ▼

The above SQL statement retrieves the product name and price for all products made by vendor DLL01 as long as the price is $4 or less. The WHERE clause in this SELECT statement is made up of two conditions, and the keyword AND is used to join them. AND instructs the database management system software to return only rows that meet all the conditions specified. If a product is made by vendor DLL01, but it costs more than $4, it is not retrieved. Similarly, products that cost less than $4 that are made by a vendor other than the one specified are not to be retrieved. The output generated by this SQL statement is as follows:

Output ▼

```
prod_id     prod_price      prod_name
-------     ----------      --------------------
BNBG02      3.4900          Bird bean bag toy
BNBG01      3.4900          Fish bean bag toy
BNBG03      3.4900          Rabbit bean bag toy
```

NEW TERM: **AND**

A keyword used in a WHERE clause to specify that only rows matching all the specified conditions should be retrieved.

The example just used contained a single AND clause and was thus made up of two filter conditions. Additional filter conditions could be used as well, each separated by an AND keyword.

NOTE: **No ORDER BY Clause Specified**

In the interests of saving space (and your typing), I omitted the ORDER BY clause in many of these examples. As such, it is entirely possible that your output won't exactly match the output in the book. While the number of returned rows should always match, their order may not. Of course, feel free to add an ORDER BY clause if you'd like; it needs to go after the WHERE clause.

Using the OR Operator

The OR operator is exactly the opposite of AND. The OR operator instructs the database management system software to retrieve rows that match either condition. In fact, most of the better DBMSs will not even evaluate the second condition in an OR WHERE clause if the first condition has already been met. (If the first condition was met, the row would be retrieved regardless of the second condition.)

Look at the following SELECT statement:

Input ▼

```
SELECT prod_id, prod_price, prod_name
FROM Products
WHERE vend_id = 'DLL01' OR vend_id = 'BRS01';
```

Analysis ▼

The above SQL statement retrieves the product name and price for any products
made by either of the two specified vendors. The OR operator tells the DBMS to
match either condition, not both. If an AND operator were used here, no data would be
returned (as it would create a WHERE clause that would match no rows). The output
generated by this SQL statement is as follows:

Output ▼

```
prod_name                  prod_price
------------------         ----------
Fish bean bag toy          3.4900
Bird bean bag toy          3.4900
Rabbit bean bag toy        3.4900
8 inch teddy bear          5.9900
12 inch teddy bear         8.9900
18 inch teddy bear         11.9900
Raggedy Ann                4.9900
```

> NEW TERM: OR
>
> A keyword used in a WHERE clause to specify that any rows matching either of
> the specified conditions should be retrieved.

Understanding Order of Evaluation

WHERE clauses can contain any number of AND and OR operators. Combining the two
enables you to perform sophisticated and complex filtering.

But combining AND and OR operators presents an interesting problem. To demonstrate
this, look at an example. You need a list of all products costing $10 or more made by
vendors DLL01 and BRS01. The following SELECT statement uses a combination of AND
and OR operators to build a WHERE clause:

Input ▼

```
SELECT prod_name, prod_price
FROM Products
WHERE vend_id = 'DLL01' OR vend_id = 'BRS01'
      AND prod_price >= 10;
```

Output ▼

```
prod_name                prod_price
-------------------      ----------
Fish bean bag toy        3.4900
Bird bean bag toy        3.4900
Rabbit bean bag toy      3.4900
18 inch teddy bear       11.9900
Raggedy Ann              4.9900
```

Analysis ▼

Look at the results above. Four of the rows returned have prices less than $10—so, obviously, the rows were not filtered as intended. Why did this happen? The answer is the order of evaluation. SQL (like most languages) processes AND operators before OR operators. When SQL sees the above WHERE clause, it reads *any products costing $10 or more made by vendor* BRS01, *and any products made by vendor* DLL01 *regardless of price*. In other words, because AND ranks higher in the order of evaluation, the wrong operators were joined together.

The solution to this problem is to use parentheses to explicitly group related operators. Take a look at the following SELECT statement and output:

Input ▼

```
SELECT prod_name, prod_price
FROM Products
WHERE (vend_id = 'DLL01' OR vend_id = 'BRS01')
      AND prod_price >= 10;
```

Output ▼

```
prod_name                prod_price
-------------------      ----------
18 inch teddy bear       11.9900
```

Analysis ▼

The only difference between this SELECT statement and the earlier one is that, in this statement, the first two WHERE clause conditions are enclosed within parentheses. As parentheses have a higher order of evaluation than either AND or OR operators, the DBMS first filters the OR condition within those parentheses. The SQL statement then becomes *any products made by either vendor* DLL01 *or vendor* BRS01 *costing $10 or greater*, which is exactly what we want.

Using the IN Operator

The IN operator is used to specify a range of conditions, any of which can be matched. IN takes a comma-delimited list of valid values, all enclosed within parentheses. The following example demonstrates this:

Input ▼

```
SELECT prod_name, prod_price
FROM Products
WHERE vend_id  IN ('DLL01','BRS01')
ORDER BY prod_name;
```

Output ▼

```
prod_name                 prod_price
--------------------      ----------
12 inch teddy bear        8.9900
18 inch teddy bear        11.9900
8 inch teddy bear         5.9900
Bird bean bag toy         3.4900
Fish bean bag toy         3.4900
Rabbit bean bag toy       3.4900
Raggedy Ann               4.9900
```

Analysis ▼

The SELECT statement retrieves all products made by vendor DLL01 and vendor BRS01. The IN operator is followed by a comma-delimited list of valid values, and the entire list must be enclosed within parentheses.

If you are thinking that the IN operator accomplishes the same goal as OR, you are right. The following SQL statement accomplishes the exact same thing as the example above:

Input ▼

```
SELECT prod_name, prod_price
FROM Products
WHERE vend_id  = 'DLL01' OR vend_id = 'BRS01'
ORDER BY prod_name;
```

Output ▼

```
prod_name           prod_price
-----------------   ----------
12 inch teddy bear  8.9900
18 inch teddy bear  11.9900
8 inch teddy bear   5.9900
Bird bean bag toy   3.4900
Fish bean bag toy   3.4900
Rabbit bean bag toy 3.4900
Raggedy Ann         4.9900
```

Why use the IN operator? The advantages are

▶ When you are working with long lists of valid options, the IN operator syntax is far cleaner and easier to read.

▶ The order of evaluation is easier to manage when IN is used in conjunction with other AND and OR operators.

▶ IN operators almost always execute more quickly than lists of OR operators (although you'll not see any performance difference with very short lists like the ones we're using here).

▶ The biggest advantage of IN is that the IN operator can contain another SELECT statement, enabling you to build highly dynamic WHERE clauses. You'll look at this in detail in Lesson 11, "Working with Subqueries."

NEW TERM: **IN**
A keyword used in a WHERE clause to specify a list of values to be matched using an OR comparison.

Using the NOT Operator

The WHERE clause's NOT operator has one function and one function only: NOT negates whatever condition comes next. Because NOT is never used by itself (it is always used in conjunction with some other operator), its syntax is a little different from all other operators. Unlike other operators, the NOT keyword can be used before the column to filter on, not just after it.

NEW TERM: **NOT**
A keyword used in a WHERE clause to negate a condition.

The following example demonstrates the use of NOT. To list the products made by all vendors except vendor DLL01, you can write the following:

Input ▼

```
SELECT prod_name
FROM Products
WHERE NOT vend_id = 'DLL01'
ORDER BY prod_name;
```

Output ▼

```
prod_name
------------------
12 inch teddy bear
18 inch teddy bear
8 inch teddy bear
King doll
Queen doll
```

Analysis ▼

The NOT here negates the condition that follows it; so instead of matching vend_id to DLL01, the DBMS matches vend_id to anything that is not DLL01.

The preceding example also could have been accomplished using the <> operator, as follows:

Input ▼

```
SELECT prod_name
FROM Products
WHERE vend_id  <> 'DLL01'
ORDER BY prod_name;
```

Output ▼

```
prod_name
------------------
12 inch teddy bear
18 inch teddy bear
8 inch teddy bear
King doll
Queen doll
```

Analysis ▼

Why use NOT? Well, for simple WHERE clauses such as the ones shown here, there really is no advantage to using NOT. NOT is useful in more complex clauses. For example, using NOT in conjunction with an IN operator makes it simple to find all rows that do not match a list of criteria.

NOTE: NOT **in MariaDB**

MariaDB supports the use of NOT to negate IN, BETWEEN, and EXISTS clauses. This is different from most DBMSs that allow NOT to be used to negate any conditions.

Summary

This lesson picked up where the last lesson left off and taught you how to combine WHERE clauses with the AND and OR operators. You also learned how to explicitly manage the order of evaluation and how to use the IN and NOT operators.

Challenges

1. Write a SQL statement to retrieve the vendor name (vend_name) from the Vendors table, returning only vendors in California (this requires filtering by both country [USA] and state [CA]; after all, there could be a California outside of the USA). Here's a hint: the filter requires matching strings.

2. Write a SQL statement to find all orders where at least 100 of items BR01, BR02, or BR03 were ordered. You'll want to return order number (order_num), product ID (prod_id), and quantity for the OrderItems table, filtering by both the product ID and quantity. Here's a hint: depending on how you write your filter, you may need to pay special attention to order of evaluation.

3. Now let's revisit a challenge from the previous lesson. Write a SQL statement that returns the product name (prod_name) and price (prod_price) from Products for all products priced between 3 and 6. Use an AND, and sort the results by price.

4. What is wrong with the following SQL statement? (Try to figure it out without running it.)

```
SELECT vend_name
FROM Vendors
ORDER BY vend_name
WHERE vend_country = 'USA' AND vend_state = 'CA';
```

Using Wildcard Filtering

In this lesson, you'll learn what wildcards are, how they are used, and how to perform wildcard searches using the LIKE *operator for sophisticated filtering of retrieved data.*

Using the LIKE Operator

All the previous operators we studied filter against known values. Be it matching one or more values, testing for greater-than or less-than known values, or checking a range of values, the common denominator is that the values used in the filtering are known.

But filtering data that way does not always work. For example, how could you search for all products that contained the text *bean bag* within the product name? That cannot be done with simple comparison operators; that's a job for wildcard searching. Using wildcards, you can create search patterns that can be compared against your data. In this example, if you want to find all products that contain the words *bean bag*, you can construct a wildcard search pattern enabling you to find that *bean bag* text anywhere within a product name.

> NEW TERM: **Wildcards**
> Special characters used to match parts of a value.

> NEW TERM: **Search pattern**
> A search condition made up of literal text, wildcard characters, or any combination of the above.

The wildcards themselves are actually characters that have special meanings within SQL WHERE clauses, and SQL supports several different wildcard types.

To use wildcards in search clauses, you must use the LIKE operator. LIKE instructs the DBMS that the following search pattern is to be compared using a wildcard match rather than a straight equality match.

Wildcard searching can only be used with text fields (strings); you can't use wildcards to search fields of nontext datatypes.

The Percent Sign (%) Wildcard

The most frequently used wildcard is the percent sign (%). Within a search string, % means *match any number of occurrences of any character*. For example, to find all products that start with the word Fish, you can issue the following SELECT statement:

Input ▼

```
SELECT prod_id, prod_name
FROM Products
WHERE prod_name LIKE 'Fish%';
```

Output ▼

```
prod_id    prod_name
-------    ------------------
BNBG01     Fish bean bag toy
```

Analysis ▼

This example uses a search pattern of 'Fish%'. When this clause is evaluated, any value that starts with Fish will be retrieved. The % tells the DBMS to accept any characters after the word Fish, regardless of how many characters there are.

NOTE: **Case Sensitivity**

Depending on our DBMS and how it is configured, searches may be case sensitive, in which case 'fish%' would not match Fish bean bag toy.

Wildcards can be used anywhere within the search pattern, and multiple wildcards may be used as well. The following example uses two wildcards, one at either end of the pattern:

Input ▼

```
SELECT prod_id, prod_name
FROM Products
WHERE prod_name LIKE '%bean bag%';
```

Output ▼

```
prod_id      prod_name
--------     --------------------
BNBG01       Fish bean bag toy
BNBG02       Bird bean bag toy
BNBG03       Rabbit bean bag toy
```

Analysis ▼

The search pattern '%bean bag%' means *match any value that contains the text* bean bag *anywhere within it, regardless of any characters before or after that text.*

Wildcards can also be used in the middle of a search pattern, although that is rarely useful. The following example finds all products that begin with an F and end with a y.

Input ▼

```
SELECT prod_name
FROM Products
WHERE prod_name LIKE 'F%y';
```

TIP: **Searching for Partial Email Addresses**

There is one situation in which wildcards may indeed be useful in the middle of a search pattern, and that is looking for email addresses based on a partial address, such as WHERE email 'LIKE b%@forta.com'.

It is important to note that, in addition to matching one or more characters, % also matches *zero* characters. % represents zero, one, or more characters at the specified location in the search pattern.

> NOTE: **Watch for Trailing Spaces**
>
> Some DBMSs pad field contents with spaces. For example, if a column expects 50 characters and the text stored is `Fish bean bag toy` (17 characters), 33 spaces may be appended to the text so as to fully fill the column. This padding usually has no real impact on data and how it is used, but it could negatively affect the just-used SQL statement. The clause `WHERE prod_name LIKE 'F%y'` will only match `prod_name` if it starts with `F` and ends with `y`, and if the value is padded with spaces, then it will not end with `y` and so `Fish bean bag toy` will not be retrieved. One simple solution to this problem is to append a second `%` to the search pattern. `'F%y%'` will also match characters (or spaces) after the `y`. A better solution would be to trim the spaces using functions, as you will learn in Lesson 8, "Using Data Manipulation Functions."

> CAUTION: **Watch for NULL**
>
> It may seem that the `%` wildcard matches anything, but there is one exception: `NULL`. Not even the clause `WHERE prod_name LIKE '%'` will match a row with the value `NULL` as the product name.

The Underscore (_) Wildcard

Another useful wildcard is the underscore (_). The underscore is used just like `%`, but instead of matching multiple characters, the underscore matches just a single character.

> NOTE: **DB2 Wildcards**
>
> The _ wildcard is not supported by DB2.

Take a look at this example:

Input ▼

```
SELECT prod_id, prod_name
FROM Products
WHERE prod_name LIKE '__ inch teddy bear';
```

> NOTE: **Watch for Trailing Spaces**
>
> As in the previous example, you may have to append a wildcard to the pattern for this example to work.

Output ▼

```
prod_id     prod_name
--------    --------------------
BR02        12 inch teddy bear
BR03        18 inch teddy bear
```

Analysis ▼

The search pattern used in this WHERE clause specified two wildcards followed by literal text. The results shown are the only rows that match the search pattern: the underscore matches 12 in the first row and 18 in the second row. The 8 inch teddy bear product did not match because the search pattern required two wildcard matches, not one. By contrast, the following SELECT statement uses the % wildcard and returns three matching products:

Input ▼

```
SELECT prod_id, prod_name
FROM Products
WHERE prod_name LIKE '% inch teddy bear';
```

Output ▼

```
prod_id     prod_name
--------    --------------------
BR01        8 inch teddy bear
BR02        12 inch teddy bear
BNR3        18 inch teddy bear
```

Unlike %, which can match zero characters, _ always matches one character—no more and no less.

The Brackets ([]) Wildcard

The brackets ([]) wildcard is used to specify a set of characters, any one of which must match a character in the specified position (the location of the wildcard).

> NOTE: **Sets Are Not Commonly Supported**
>
> Unlike the wildcards described thus far, the use of [] to create sets is not supported by all DBMSs. Sets are supported in Microsoft SQL Server, but are not supported in MySQL, Oracle, DB2, and SQLite. Consult your DBMS documentation to determine if sets are supported.

For example, to find all contacts whose names begin with the letter J or the letter M, you can do the following:

Input ▼

```
SELECT cust_contact
FROM Customers
WHERE cust_contact LIKE '[JM]%'
ORDER BY cust_contact;
```

Output ▼

```
cust_contact
-----------------
Jim Jones
John Smith
Michelle Green
```

Analysis ▼

The WHERE clause in this statement is '[JM]%'. This search pattern uses two different wildcards. The [JM] matches any contact name that begins with either of the letters within the brackets, and it also matches only a single character. Therefore, any names longer than one character will not match. The % wildcard after the [JM] matches any number of characters after the first character, returning the desired results.

This wildcard can be negated by prefixing the characters with ^ (the caret character). For example, the following matches any contact name that does not begin with the letter J or the letter M (the opposite of the previous example):

Input ▼

```
SELECT cust_contact
FROM Customers
WHERE cust_contact LIKE '[^JM]%'
ORDER BY cust_contact;
```

Of course, you can accomplish the same result using the NOT operator. The only advantage of ^ is that it can simplify the syntax if you are using multiple WHERE clauses:

Input ▼

```
SELECT cust_contact
FROM Customers
WHERE NOT cust_contact LIKE '[JM]%'
ORDER BY cust_contact;
```

Tips for Using Wildcards

As you can see, SQL's wildcards are extremely powerful. But that power comes with a price: wildcard searches typically take far longer to process than any other search types discussed previously. Here are some rules to keep in mind when using wildcards:

- ▶ Don't overuse wildcards. If another search operator will do, use it instead.

- ▶ When you do use wildcards, try not to use them at the beginning of the search pattern unless absolutely necessary. Search patterns that begin with wildcards are the slowest to process.

- ▶ Pay careful attention to the placement of the wildcard symbols. If they are misplaced, you might not return the data you intended.

Having said that, wildcards are an important and useful search tool, and one that you will use frequently.

Summary

In this lesson, you learned what wildcards are and how to use SQL wildcards within your WHERE clauses. You also learned that wildcards should be used carefully and never overused.

Challenges

1. Write a SQL statement to retrieve the product name (prod_name) and description (prod_desc) from the Products table, returning only products where the word toy is in the description.

2. Now let's flip things around. Write a SQL statement to retrieve the product name (prod_name) and description (prod_desc) from the Products table, returning only products where the word toy doesn't appear in the description. And this time, sort the results by product name.

3. Write a SQL statement to retrieve the product name (prod_name) and description (prod_desc) from the Products table, returning only products where both the words toy and carrots appear in the description. There are a couple of ways to do this, but for this challenge use AND and two LIKE comparisons.

4. This next one is a little trickier. I didn't show you this syntax specifically, but see whether you can figure it out anyway based on what you have learned thus far. Write a SQL statement to retrieve the product name (prod_name) and description (prod_desc) from the Products table, returning only products where both the words toy and carrots appear in the description in that order (the word toy before the word carrots). Here's a hint: you'll only need one LIKE with three % symbols to do this.

LESSON 7

Creating Calculated Fields

In this lesson, you will learn what calculated fields are, how to create them, and how to use aliases to refer to them from within your application.

Understanding Calculated Fields

Data stored within a database's tables is often not available in the exact format needed by your applications. Here are some examples:

▶ You need to display a field containing the name of a company along with the company's location, but that information is stored in separate table columns.

▶ City, state, and ZIP codes are stored in separate columns (as they should be), but your mailing label printing program needs them retrieved as one correctly formatted field.

▶ Column data is in mixed upper- and lowercase, and your report needs all data presented in uppercase.

▶ An OrderItems table stores item price and quantity, but not the expanded price (price multiplied by quantity) of each item. To print invoices, you need that expanded price.

▶ You need total, averages, or other calculations based on table data.

In each of these examples, the data stored in the table is not exactly what your application needs. Rather than retrieve the data as it is and then reformat it within your client application or report, what you really want is to retrieve converted, calculated, or reformatted data directly from the database.

This is where calculated fields come in. Unlike all the columns that we have retrieved in the lessons thus far, calculated fields don't actually exist in database tables. Rather, a calculated field is created on-the-fly within a SQL SELECT statement.

> NEW TERM: **Field**
> Essentially means the same thing as *column* and often used interchangeably, although database columns are typically called *columns* and the term *fields* is usually used in conjunction with calculated fields.

It is important to note that only the database knows which columns in a SELECT statement are actual table columns and which are calculated fields. From the perspective of a client (for example, your application), a calculated field's data is returned in the same way as data from any other column.

> TIP: **Client Versus Server Formatting**
> Many of the conversions and reformatting that can be performed within SQL statements can also be performed directly in your client application. However, as a rule, it is far quicker to perform these operations on the database server than it is to perform them within the client.

Concatenating Fields

To demonstrate working with calculated fields, let's start with a simple example—creating a title that is made up of two columns.

The Vendors table contains vendor name and address information. Imagine that you are generating a vendor report and need to list the vendor location as part of the vendor name, in the format name (location).

The report wants a single value, and the data in the table is stored in two columns: vend_name and vend_country. In addition, you need to surround vend_country with parentheses, and those are definitely not stored in the database table. The SELECT statement that returns the vendor names and locations is simple enough, but how would you create this combined value?

> NEW TERM: **Concatenate**
> Joining values together (by appending them to each other) to form a single long value.

The solution is to concatenate the two columns. In SQL SELECT statements, you can concatenate columns using a special operator. Depending on what DBMS you are using, this operator can be a plus sign (+) or two pipes (||). And in the case of MySQL and MariaDB, a special function must be used as seen below.

Here's an example using the plus sign:

Input ▼

```
SELECT vend_name + '(' + vend_country + ')'
FROM Vendors
ORDER BY vend_name;
```

Output ▼

```
------------------------------------------------------------
Bear Emporium                  (USA                )
Bears R Us                     (USA                )
Doll House Inc.                (USA                )
Fun and Games                  (England            )
Furball Inc.                   (USA                )
Jouets et ours                 (France             )
```

The following is the same statement, but using the || syntax:

Input ▼

```
SELECT vend_name || '(' || vend_country || ')'
FROM Vendors
ORDER BY vend_name;
```

Output ▼

```
------------------------------------------------------------
Bear Emporium                  (USA                )
Bears R Us                     (USA                )
Doll House Inc.                (USA                )
Fun and Games                  (England            )
Furball Inc.                   (USA                )
Jouets et ours                 (France             )
```

And here's what you'll need to do if using MySQL or MariaDB:

Input ▼

```
SELECT Concat(vend_name, ' (', vend_country, ')')
FROM Vendors
ORDER BY vend_name;
```

Analysis ▼

The above SELECT statements concatenate the following elements:

▶ The name stored in the vend_name column

▶ A string containing a space and an open parenthesis

▶ The country stored in the vend_country column

▶ A string containing the close parenthesis

As you can see in the output shown above, the SELECT statement returns a single column (a calculated field) containing all these four elements as one unit.

Look again at the output returned by the SELECT statement. The two columns that are incorporated into the calculated field are padded with spaces. Many databases (although not all) save text values padded to the column width, so your own results may indeed not contain those extraneous spaces. To return the data formatted properly, you must trim those padded spaces. This can be done using the SQL RTRIM() function, as follows:

Input ▼

```
SELECT RTRIM(vend_name) + ' (' + RTRIM(vend_country) + ')'
FROM Vendors
ORDER BY vend_name;
```

Output ▼

```
------------------------------------------------------------
Bear Emporium (USA)
Bears R Us (USA)
Doll House Inc. (USA)
Fun and Games (England)
Furball Inc. (USA)
Jouets et ours (France)
```

The following is the same statement, but using the || syntax:

Input ▼

```
SELECT RTRIM(vend_name) || ' (' || RTRIM(vend_country) || ')'
FROM Vendors
ORDER BY vend_name;
```

Output ▼

```
- - - - - - - - - - - - - - - - - - - - - - - - - - - - - - - - - - - - - - - - - - - - - - - - - - -
Bear Emporium (USA)
Bears R Us (USA)
Doll House Inc. (USA)
Fun and Games (England)
Furball Inc. (USA)
Jouets et ours (France)
```

Analysis ▼

The RTRIM() function trims all space from the right of a value. When you use RTRIM(), the individual columns are all trimmed properly.

> NOTE: **The TRIM Functions**
>
> Most DBMSs support RTRIM() (which, as just seen, trims the right side of a string), as well as LTRIM(), which trims the left side of a string, and TRIM(), which trims both the right and left.

Using Aliases

The SELECT statement used to concatenate the address field works well, as seen in the above output. But what is the name of this new calculated column? Well, the truth is, it has no name; it is simply a value. Although this can be fine if you are just looking at the results in a SQL query tool, an unnamed column cannot be used within a client application because there is no way for the client to refer to that column.

To solve this problem, SQL supports column aliases. An alias is just that, an alternate name for a field or value. Aliases are assigned with the AS keyword. Take a look at the following SELECT statement:

Input ▼

```
SELECT RTRIM(vend_name) + ' (' + RTRIM(vend_country) + ')'
 AS vend_title
FROM Vendors
ORDER BY vend_name;
```

Output ▼

```
vend_title
--------------------------------------------------------------
Bear Emporium (USA)
Bears R Us (USA)
Doll House Inc. (USA)
Fun and Games (England)
Furball Inc. (USA)
Jouets et ours (France)
```

The following is the same statement, but using the || syntax:

Input ▼

```
SELECT RTRIM(vend_name) || ' (' || RTRIM(vend_country) || ')'
  AS vend_title
FROM Vendors
ORDER BY vend_name;
```

And here is the equivalent for use with MySQL and MariaDB:

Input ▼

```
SELECT Concat(RTrim(vend_name), ' (',
       RTrim(vend_country), ')') AS vend_title
FROM Vendors
ORDER BY vend_name;
```

Analysis ▼

The SELECT statement itself is the same as the one used in the previous code snippet, except that here the calculated field is followed by the text AS vend_title. This instructs SQL to create a calculated field named vend_title containing the calculation specified. As you can see in the output, the results are the same as before, but the column is now named vend_title, and any client application can refer to this column by name, just as it would to any actual table column.

> **NOTE: AS Often Optional**
> Use of the AS keyword is optional in many DBMSs, but using it is considered a best practice.

> TIP: **Other Uses for Aliases**
>
> Aliases have other uses too. Some common uses include renaming a column if the real table column name contains illegal characters (for example, spaces) and expanding column names if the original names are either ambiguous or easily misread.

> CAUTION: **Alias Names**
>
> Aliases may be single words or complete strings. If the latter is used, then the string should be enclosed within quotes. This practice is legal but is strongly discouraged. While multiword names are indeed highly readable, they create all sorts of problems for many client applications—so much so that one of the most common uses of aliases is to rename multiword column names to single-word names (as explained above).

> NOTE: **Derived Columns**
>
> Aliases are also sometimes referred to as `derived columns`, so regardless of the term you run across, they mean the same thing.

Performing Mathematical Calculations

Another frequent use for calculated fields is performing mathematical calculations on retrieved data. Let's take a look at an example. The `Orders` table contains all orders received, and the `OrderItems` table contains the individual items within each order. The following SQL statement retrieves all the items in order number `20008`:

Input ▼

```
SELECT prod_id, quantity, item_price
FROM OrderItems
WHERE order_num = 20008;
```

Output ▼

```
prod_id     quantity      item_price
----------  -----------   ---------------------
RGAN01      5             4.9900
BR03        5             11.9900
BNBG01      10            3.4900
BNBG02      10            3.4900
BNBG03      10            3.4900
```

The item_price column contains the per unit price for each item in an order. To expand the item price (item price multiplied by quantity ordered), you simply do the following:

Input ▼

```
SELECT prod_id,
       quantity,
       item_price,
       quantity*item_price AS expanded_price
FROM OrderItems
WHERE order_num = 20008;
```

Output ▼

prod_id	quantity	item_price	expanded_price
RGAN01	5	4.9900	24.9500
BR03	5	11.9900	59.9500
BNBG01	10	3.4900	34.9000
BNBG02	10	3.4900	34.9000
BNBG03	10	3.4900	34.9000

Analysis ▼

The expanded_price column shown in the output above is a calculated field; the calculation is simply quantity*item_price. The client application can now use this new calculated column just as it would any other column.

SQL supports the basic mathematical operators listed in Table 7.1. In addition, you can use parentheses to establish order of precedence. Refer to Lesson 5, "Advanced Data Filtering," for an explanation of precedence.

TABLE 7.1 SQL Mathematical Operators

Operator	Description
+	Addition
–	Subtraction
*	Multiplication
/	Division

> TIP: **How to Test Calculations**
>
> SELECT provides a great way to test and experiment with functions and calculations. Although SELECT is usually used to retrieve data from a table, the FROM clause may be omitted to simply access and work with expressions. For example, SELECT 3 * 2; would return 6, SELECT Trim(' abc '); would return abc, and SELECT Curdate(); uses the Curdate() function to return the current date and time (on MySQL and MariaDB, for example). You get the idea: use SELECT to experiment as needed.

Summary

In this lesson, you learned what calculated fields are and how to create them. You used examples demonstrating the use of calculated fields for both string concatenation and mathematical operations. In addition, you learned how to create and use aliases so that your application can refer to calculated fields.

Challenges

1. A common use for aliases is to rename table column fields in retrieved results (perhaps to match specific reporting or client needs). Write a SQL statement that retrieves vend_id, vend_name, vend_address, and vend_city from Vendors, renaming vend_name to vname, vend_city to vcity, and vend_address to vaddress. Sort the results by vendor name (you can use the original name or the renamed name).

2. Our example store is running a sale and all products are 10% off. Write a SQL statement that returns prod_id, prod_price, and sale_price from the Products table. sale_price is a calculated field that contains, well, the sale price. Here's a hint: you can multiply by 0.9 to get 90% of the original value (and thus the 10% off price).

Using Data Manipulation Functions

In this lesson, you'll learn what functions are, what types of functions DBMSs support, and how to use these functions. You'll also learn why SQL function use can be very problematic.

Understanding Functions

Like almost any other computer language, SQL supports the use of functions to manipulate data. Functions are operations that are usually performed on data, usually to facilitate conversion and manipulation, and they are an important part of your SQL toolbox.

An example of a function is `RTRIM()`, which we used in the last lesson to trim spaces from the end of a string.

The Problem with Functions

Before you work through this lesson and try the examples, you should be aware that, unfortunately, using SQL functions can be highly problematic.

Unlike SQL statements (for example, `SELECT`), which for the most part are supported by all DBMSs equally, functions tend to be very DBMS specific. In fact, very few functions are supported identically by all major DBMSs. Although all types of functionality are usually available in each DBMS, the function names or syntax can differ greatly. To demonstrate just how problematic this can be, Table 8.1 lists three commonly needed functions and their syntax as employed by various DBMSs:

TABLE 8.1   DBMS Function Differences

Function	Syntax
Extract part of a string	DB2, Oracle, PostgreSQL, and SQLite use `SUBSTR()`. MariaDB, MySQL, and SQL Server use `SUBSTRING()`.
Datatype conversion	Oracle uses multiple functions, one for each conversion type. DB2, PostgreSQL, and SQL Server use `CAST()`. MariaDB, MySQL, and SQL Server use `CONVERT()`.
Get current date	DB2 and PostgreSQL use `CURRENT_DATE`. MariaDB and MySQL use `CURDATE()`. Oracle uses `SYSDATE`. SQL Server uses `GETDATE()`. SQLite uses `DATE()`.

As you can see, unlike SQL statements, SQL functions are not *portable*. This means that code you write for a specific SQL implementation might not work on another implementation.

NEW TERM: **Portable**

Code that is written so that it will run on multiple different systems.

With code portability in mind, some SQL programmers opt not to use any implementation-specific features. Although this is a somewhat noble and idealistic view, it is not always in the best interests of application performance. If you opt not to use these functions, you make your application code work harder, as it must use other methods to do what the DBMS could have done more efficiently.

TIP: **Should You Use Functions?**

So now you are trying to decide whether you should or shouldn't use functions. Well, that decision is yours, and there is no right or wrong choice. If you do decide to use functions, make sure you comment your code well so that at a later date you (or another developer) will know exactly what SQL implementation you were writing to.

Using Functions

Most SQL implementations support the following types of functions:

▶ Text functions are used to manipulate strings of text (for example, trimming or padding values and converting values to upper- and lowercase).

▶ Numeric functions are used to perform mathematical operations on numeric data (for example, returning absolute numbers and performing algebraic calculations).

▶ Date and time functions are used to manipulate date and time values and to extract specific components from these values (for example, returning differences between dates and checking date validity).

▶ Formatting functions are used to generate user-friendly outputs (for example, displaying dates in local languages and formats, or currencies with the right symbols and comma placement).

▶ System functions return information specific to the DBMS being used (for example, returning user login information).

In the last lesson, you saw a function used as part of a column list in a SELECT statement, but that's not all functions can do. You can use functions in other parts of the SELECT statement (for instance, in the WHERE clause), as well as in other SQL statements (more on that in later lessons).

Text Manipulation Functions

You've already seen an example of text manipulation functions: in the last lesson, the RTRIM() function was used to trim white space from the end of a column value. Here is another example, this time using the UPPER() function:

Input ▼

```
SELECT vend_name, UPPER(vend_name) AS vend_name_upcase
FROM Vendors
ORDER BY vend_name;
```

Output ▼

vend_name	vend_name_upcase
Bear Emporium	BEAR EMPORIUM
Bears R Us	BEARS R US
Doll House Inc.	DOLL HOUSE INC.
Fun and Games	FUN AND GAMES
Furball Inc.	FURBALL INC.
Jouets et ours	JOUETS ET OURS

As you can see, UPPER() converts text to uppercase, and so in this example each vendor is listed twice—first exactly as stored in the Vendors table, and then converted to uppercase as column vend_name_upcase.

> **TIP: UPPERCASE, lowercase, MixedCase**
> As should be clear by now, SQL functions are not case sensitive, so you can use upper(), UPPER(), Upper(), or substr(), SUBSTR(), SubStr(), and so on. Case is a user preference, so do as you choose, but be consistent and don't keep changing styles in your code; it makes the SQL really hard to read.

Table 8.2 lists some commonly used text manipulation functions.

TABLE 8.2 Commonly Used Text Manipulation Functions

Function	Description
LEFT() (or use substring function	Returns characters from left of string
LENGTH() (also DATALENGTH() or LEN())	Returns the length of a string
LOWER()	Converts string to lowercase
LTRIM()	Trims white space from left of string
RIGHT() (or use substring function)	Returns characters from right of string
RTRIM()	Trims white space from right of string
SUBSTR() or SUBSTRING()	Extracts part of a string (as noted in Table 8.1)
SOUNDEX()	Returns a string's SOUNDEX value
UPPER()	Converts string to uppercase

One item in Table 8.2 requires further explanation. SOUNDEX is an algorithm that converts any string of text into an alphanumeric pattern describing the phonetic representation of that text. SOUNDEX takes into account similar-sounding characters and syllables, enabling strings to be compared by how they sound rather than how they have been typed. Although SOUNDEX is not a SQL concept, most DBMSs do offer SOUNDEX support.

> **NOTE: SOUNDEX Support**
>
> SOUNDEX() is not supported by PostgreSQL, and so the following example will not work on that DBMS.
>
> In addition, it is only available in SQLite if the SQLITE_SOUNDEX compile-time option is used when SQLite is built, and as this is not the default compile option, most SQLite implementations won't support SOUNDEX().

Here's an example using the SOUNDEX() function. Customer Kids Place is in the Customers table and has a contact named Michelle Green. But what if that were a typo, and the contact actually was supposed to have been Michael Green? Obviously, searching by the correct contact name would return no data, as shown here:

Input ▼

```
SELECT cust_name, cust_contact
FROM Customers
WHERE cust_contact = 'Michael Green';
```

Output ▼

```
cust_name                    cust_contact
-----------------------      ---------------------------
```

Now try the same search using the SOUNDEX() function to match all contact names that sound similar to Michael Green:

Input ▼

```
SELECT cust_name, cust_contact
FROM Customers
WHERE SOUNDEX(cust_contact) = SOUNDEX('Michael Green');
```

Output ▼

```
cust_name                    cust_contact
-----------------------      ---------------------------
Kids Place                   Michelle Green
```

Analysis ▼

In this example, the WHERE clause uses the SOUNDEX() function to convert both the cust_contact column value and the search string to their SOUNDEX values. Because Michael Green and Michelle Green sound alike, their SOUNDEX values match, and so the WHERE clause correctly filtered the desired data.

Date and Time Manipulation Functions

Date and times are stored in tables using datatypes, and each DBMS uses its own special varieties. Date and time values are stored in special formats so that they may be sorted or filtered quickly and efficiently, as well as to save physical storage space.

The internal format used to store dates and times is usually of no use to your applications, and so date and time functions are almost always used to read, expand, and manipulate these values. Because of this, date and time manipulation functions are some of the most important functions in the SQL language. Unfortunately, they also tend to be the most inconsistent and least portable.

To demonstrate the use of a date manipulation function, here is a simple example. The Orders table contains all orders along with an order date. To retrieve all of the orders placed in a specific year, you'd need to filter by order date, but not the entire date value, just the year portion of it. This obviously necessitates extracting the year from the complete date.

To retrieve a list of all orders made in 2020 in SQL Server, do the following:

Input ▼

```
SELECT order_num
FROM Orders
WHERE DATEPART(yy, order_date) = 2020;
```

Output ▼

```
order_num
-----------
20005
20006
20007
20008
20009
```

Analysis ▼

This example uses the DATEPART() function, which, as its name suggests, returns a part of a date. DATEPART() takes two parameters: the part to return and the date to return it from. In our example DATEPART() specifies yy as the desired part and returns just the year from the order_date column. By comparing that to 2020, the WHERE clause can filter just the orders for that year.

Here is the PostgreSQL version, which uses a similar function named DATE_PART():

Input ▼

```
SELECT order_num
FROM Orders
WHERE DATE_PART('year', order_date) = 2020;
```

Oracle has no DATEPART() function either, but there are several other date manipulation functions that can be used to accomplish the same retrieval. Here is an example:

Input ▼

```
SELECT order_num
FROM Orders
WHERE EXTRACT(year FROM order_date) = 2020;
```

Analysis ▼

In this example, the EXTRACT() function is used to extract part of the date with year specifying what part of the date to extract. The returned value is then compared to 2020.

> TIP: **PostgreSQL Supports Extract()**
> PostgreSQL also supports the Extract() function, so this technique will work (in addition to using DatePart() as seen previously).

Another way to accomplish this same task is to use the BETWEEN operator:

Input ▼

```
SELECT order_num
FROM Orders
WHERE order_date BETWEEN to_date('2020-01-01', 'yyyy-mm-dd')
 AND to_date('2020-12-31', 'yyyy-mm-dd');
```

Analysis ▼

In this example, Oracle's to_date() function is used to convert two strings to dates. One contains the date January 1, 2020, and the other contains the date December 31, 2020. A standard BETWEEN operator is used to find all orders between those two dates. It is worth noting that this same code would not work with SQL Server because it does not support the to_date() function. However, if you replaced to_date() with DATEPART(), you could indeed use this type of statement.

DB2, MySQL, and MariaDB have all sorts of date manipulation functions, but not DATEPART(). DB2, MySQL, and MariaDB users can use a function named YEAR() to extract the year from a date:

Input ▼

```
SELECT order_num
FROM Orders
WHERE YEAR(order_date) = 2020;
```

SQLite is a little trickier:

Input ▼

```
SELECT order_num
FROM Orders
WHERE strftime('%Y', order_date) = '2020';
```

The example shown here extracted and used part of a date (the year). To filter by a specific month, you could use the same process, specifying an AND operator and both year and month comparisons.

DBMSs typically offer far more than simple date part extraction. Most have functions for comparing dates, performing date-based arithmetic, formatting dates, and more. But, as you have seen, date-time manipulation functions are particularly DBMS specific. Refer to your DBMS documentation for the list of the date-time manipulation functions it supports.

Numeric Manipulation Functions

Numeric manipulation functions do just that—manipulate numeric data. These functions tend to be used primarily for algebraic, trigonometric, or geometric calculations and, therefore, are not as frequently used as string or date and time manipulation functions.

The ironic thing is that of all the functions found in the major DBMSs, the numeric functions are the ones that are most uniform and consistent. Table 8.3 lists some of the more commonly used numeric manipulation functions.

TABLE 8.3 Commonly Used Numeric Manipulation Functions

Function	Description
ABS()	Returns a number's absolute value
COS()	Returns the trigonometric cosine of a specified angle
EXP()	Returns the exponential value of a specific number
PI()	Returns the value of PI
SIN()	Returns the trigonometric sine of a specified angle
SQRT()	Returns the square root of a specified number
TAN()	Returns the trigonometric tangent of a specified angle

Refer to your DBMS documentation for a list of the supported mathematical manipulation functions.

Summary

In this lesson, you learned how to use SQL's data manipulation functions. You also learned that although these functions can be extremely useful in formatting, manipulating, and filtering data, the function details are very inconsistent from one SQL implementation to the next.

Challenges

1. Our store is now online, and customer accounts are being created. All users need a login, and the default login will be a combination of their name and city. Write a SQL statement that returns customer ID (`cust_id`), customer name (`customer_name`), and `user_login`, which is all uppercase and composed of the first two characters of the customer contact (`cust_contact`) and the first three characters of the customer city (`cust_city`). So, for example, my login (Ben Forta living in Oak Park) would be `BEOAK`. Hint: for this one you'll use functions, concatenation, and an alias.

2. Write a SQL statement to return the order number (`order_num`) and order date (`order_date`) for all orders placed in January 2020, sorted by order date. You should be able to figure this out based on what you have learned thus far, but feel free to consult your DBMS documentation as needed.

LESSON 9

Summarizing Data

In this lesson, you will learn what the SQL aggregate functions are and how to use them to summarize table data.

Using Aggregate Functions

It is often necessary to summarize data without actually retrieving it all, and SQL provides special functions for this purpose. Using these functions, SQL queries are often used to retrieve data for analysis and reporting purposes. Examples of this type of retrieval are

- ▶ Determining the number of rows in a table (or the number of rows that meet some condition or contain a specific value)

- ▶ Obtaining the sum of a set of rows in a table

- ▶ Finding the highest, lowest, and average values in a table column (either for all rows or for specific rows)

In each of these examples, you want a summary of the data in a table, not the actual data itself. Therefore, returning the actual table data would be a waste of time and processing resources (not to mention bandwidth). To repeat, all you really want is the summary information.

To facilitate this type of retrieval, SQL features a set of five *aggregate functions*, which are listed in Table 9.1. These functions enable you to perform all the types of retrieval just enumerated. You'll be relieved to know that unlike the data manipulation functions in the last lesson, SQL's aggregate functions are supported pretty consistently by the major SQL implementations.

> NEW TERM: **Aggregate Functions**
> Functions that operate on a set of rows to calculate and return a single value.

TABLE 9.1   SQL Aggregate Functions

Function	Description
AVG()	Returns a column's average value
COUNT()	Returns the number of rows in a column
MAX()	Returns a column's highest value
MIN()	Returns a column's lowest value
SUM()	Returns the sum of a column's values

The use of each of these functions is explained in the following sections.

The AVG() Function

AVG() is used to return the average value of a specific column by counting both the number of rows in the table and the sum of their values. AVG() can be used to return the average value of all columns or of specific columns or rows.

This first example uses AVG() to return the average price of all the products in the Products table:

Input ▼

```
SELECT AVG(prod_price) AS avg_price
FROM Products;
```

Output ▼

```
avg_price
-------------
6.823333
```

Analysis ▼

The SELECT statement above returns a single value—avg_price, which contains the average price of all products in the Products table. avg_price is an alias as explained in Lesson 7, "Creating Calculated Fields."

AVG() can also be used to determine the average value of specific columns or rows. The following example returns the average price of products offered by a specific vendor:

Input ▼

```
SELECT AVG(prod_price) AS avg_price
FROM Products
WHERE vend_id = 'DLL01';
```

Output ▼

```
avg_price
-----------
3.8650
```

Analysis ▼

This SELECT statement differs from the previous one only in that this one contains a WHERE clause. The WHERE clause filters only products with a vendor_id of DLL01, and, therefore, the value returned in avg_price is the average of just that vendor's products.

CAUTION: **Individual Columns Only**

AVG() may only be used to determine the average of a specific numeric column, and that column name must be specified as the function parameter. To obtain the average value of multiple columns, you must use multiple AVG() functions. The exception to this is when returning a single value that is calculated from multiple columns, as will be explained later in this lesson.

NOTE: NULL **Values**

Column rows containing NULL values are ignored by the AVG() function.

The COUNT() **Function**

COUNT() does just that—it counts. Using COUNT(), you can determine the number of rows in a table or the number of rows that match a specific criterion.

COUNT() can be used two ways:

▶ Use COUNT(*) to count the number of rows in a table, whether columns contain values or NULL values.

▶ Use COUNT(column) to count the number of rows that have values in a specific column, ignoring NULL values.

This first example returns the total number of customers in the Customers table:

Input ▼

```
SELECT COUNT(*) AS num_cust
FROM Customers;
```

Output ▼

```
num_cust
--------
5
```

Analysis ▼

In this example, COUNT(*) is used to count all rows, regardless of values. The count is returned in num_cust.

The following example counts just the customers with an email address:

Input ▼

```
SELECT COUNT(cust_email) AS num_cust
FROM Customers;
```

Output ▼

```
num_cust
--------
3
```

Analysis ▼

This SELECT statement uses COUNT(cust_email) to count only rows with a value in the cust_email column. In this example, cust_email is 3 (meaning that only 3 of the 5 customers have email addresses).

> NOTE: NULL **Values**
> Column rows with NULL values in them are ignored by the COUNT() function if a column name is specified, but not if the asterisk (*) is used.

The MAX() **Function**

MAX() returns the highest value in a specified column. MAX() requires that the column name be specified, as seen here:

Input ▼

```
SELECT MAX(prod_price) AS max_price
FROM Products;
```

Output ▼

```
max_price
----------
11.9900
```

Analysis ▼

Here MAX() returns the price of the most expensive item in the Products table.

TIP: **Using MAX() with Nonnumeric Data**

Although MAX() is usually used to find the highest numeric or date values, many (but not all) DBMSs allow it to be used to return the highest value in any columns including textual columns. When used with textual data, MAX() returns the row that would be the last if the data were sorted by that column.

NOTE: NULL **Values**

Column rows with NULL values in them are ignored by the MAX() function.

The MIN() Function

MIN() does the exact opposite of MAX()—it returns the lowest value in a specified column. Like MAX(), MIN() requires that the column name be specified, as seen here:

Input ▼

```
SELECT MIN(prod_price) AS min_price
FROM Products;
```

Output ▼

```
min_price
----------
3.4900
```

Analysis ▼

Here MIN() returns the price of the least expensive item in the Products table.

The SUM() Function

SUM() is used to return the sum (total) of the values in a specific column.

Here is an example to demonstrate this. The OrderItems table contains the actual items in an order, and each item has an associated quantity. The total number of items ordered (the sum of all the quantity values) can be retrieved as follows:

Input ▼

```
SELECT SUM(quantity) AS items_ordered
FROM OrderItems
WHERE order_num = 20005;
```

Output ▼

```
items_ordered
----------
200
```

Analysis ▼

The function SUM(quantity) returns the sum of all the item quantities in an order, and the WHERE clause ensures that just the right order items are included.

SUM() can also be used to total calculated values. In this next example the total order amount is retrieved by totaling item_price*quantity for each item:

Input ▼

```
SELECT SUM(item_price*quantity) AS total_price
FROM OrderItems
WHERE order_num = 20005;
```

Output ▼

```
total_price
----------
1648.0000
```

Analysis ▼

The function `SUM(item_price*quantity)` returns the sum of all the expanded prices
in an order, and again the `WHERE` clause ensures that just the right order items are
included.

> TIP: **Performing Calculations on Multiple Columns**
>
> All the aggregate functions can be used to perform calculations on multiple
> columns using the standard mathematical operators, as shown in the example.

> NOTE: `NULL` **Values**
>
> Column rows with `NULL` values in them are ignored by the `SUM()` function.

Aggregates on Distinct Values

The five aggregate functions can all be used in two ways:

▶ To perform calculations on all rows, specify the `ALL` argument or specify no
argument at all (because `ALL` is the default behavior).

▶ To include only unique values, specify the `DISTINCT` argument.

> TIP: `ALL` **Is Default**
>
> The `ALL` argument need not be specified because it is the default behavior. If
> `DISTINCT` is not specified, `ALL` is assumed.

The following example uses the `AVG()` function to return the average product price
offered by a specific vendor. It is the same `SELECT` statement used above, but here the
`DISTINCT` argument is used so that the average only takes into account unique prices:

Input ▼

```
SELECT AVG(DISTINCT prod_price) AS avg_price
FROM Products
WHERE vend_id = 'DLL01';
```

Output ▼

```
avg_price
----------
4.2400
```

Analysis ▼

As you can see, in this example `avg_price` is higher when DISTINCT is used because there are multiple items with the same lower price. Excluding them raises the average price.

> CAUTION: **No** DISTINCT **with** COUNT(*)
>
> DISTINCT may only be used with COUNT() if a column name is specified. DISTINCT may not be used with COUNT(*). Similarly, DISTINCT must be used with a column name and not with a calculation or expression.

> TIP: **Using** DISTINCT **with** MIN() **and** MAX()
>
> Although DISTINCT can technically be used with MIN() and MAX(), there is actually no value in doing so. The minimum and maximum values in a column will be the same whether or not only distinct values are included.

> NOTE: **Additional Aggregate Arguments**
>
> In addition to the DISTINCT and ALL arguments shown here, some DBMSs support additional arguments such as TOP and TOP PERCENT that let you perform calculations on subsets of query results. Refer to your DBMS documentation to determine exactly what arguments are available to you.

Combining Aggregate Functions

All the examples of aggregate functions used thus far have involved a single function. But actually, SELECT statements can contain as few or as many aggregate functions as needed. Look at this example:

Input ▼

```
SELECT COUNT(*) AS num_items,
       MIN(prod_price) AS price_min,
       MAX(prod_price) AS price_max,
       AVG(prod_price) AS price_avg
FROM Products;
```

Output ▼

num_items	price_min	price_max	price_avg
9	3.4900	11.9900	6.823333

Analysis ▼

Here a single SELECT statement performs four aggregate calculations in one step and returns four values (the number of items in the Products table and the highest, lowest, and average product prices).

CAUTION: **Naming Aliases**

When specifying alias names to contain the results of an aggregate function, try to not use the name of an actual column in the table. Although there is nothing actually illegal about doing so, many SQL implementations do not support this and will generate obscure error messages if you do so.

Summary

Aggregate functions are used to summarize data. SQL supports five aggregate functions, all of which can be used in multiple ways to return just the results you need. These functions are designed to be highly efficient, and they usually return results far more quickly than you could calculate them yourself within your own client application.

Challenges

1. Write a SQL statement to determine the total number of items sold (using the quantity column in OrderItems).

2. Modify the statement you just created to determine the total number of product item (prod_item) BR01 sold.

3. Write a SQL statement to determine the price (prod_price) of the most expensive item in the Products table that costs no more than 10. Name the calculated field max_price.

LESSON 10

Grouping Data

In this lesson, you'll learn how to group data so that you can summarize subsets of table contents. This involves two new SELECT *statement clauses: the* GROUP BY *clause and the* HAVING *clause.*

Understanding Data Grouping

In the last lesson, you learned that the SQL aggregate functions can be used to summarize data. These functions enable you to count rows, calculate sums and averages, and obtain high and low values without having to retrieve all the data.

All the calculations thus far were performed on all the data in a table or on data that matched a specific WHERE clause. As a reminder, the following example returns the number of products offered by vendor DLL01:

Input ▼

```
SELECT COUNT(*) AS num_prods
FROM Products
WHERE vend_id ='DLL01';
```

Output ▼

```
num_prods
-----------
4
```

But what if you wanted to return the number of products offered by each vendor? Or products offered by vendors who offer a single product, or only those who offer more than 10 products?

This is where groups come into play. Grouping lets you divide data into logical sets so that you can perform aggregate calculations on each group.

Creating Groups

Groups are created using the GROUP BY clause in your SELECT statement. The best
way to understand this is to look at an example:

Input ▼

```
SELECT vend_id, COUNT(*) AS num_prods
FROM Products
GROUP BY vend_id;
```

Output ▼

```
vend_id   num_prods
-------   ---------
BRS01     3
DLL01     4
FNG01     2
```

Analysis ▼

The above SELECT statement specifies two columns, vend_id, which contains the ID
of a product's vendor, and num_prods, which is a calculated field (created using the
COUNT(*) function). The GROUP BY clause instructs the DBMS to sort the data and
group it by vend_id. This causes num_prods to be calculated once per vend_id rather
than once for the entire table. As you can see in the output, vendor BRS01 has
3 products listed, vendor DLL01 has 4 products listed, and vendor FNG01 has
2 products listed.

Because you used GROUP BY, you did not have to specify each group to be evaluated and calculated. That was done automatically. The GROUP BY clause instructs the
DBMS to group the data and then perform the aggregate on each group rather than on
the entire result set.

Before you use GROUP BY, here are some important rules about its use that you need
to know:

- ▶ GROUP BY clauses can contain as many columns as you want. This enables
  you to nest groups, providing you with more granular control over how data
  is grouped.

- ▶ If you have nested groups in your GROUP BY clause, data is summarized
  at the last specified group. In other words, all the columns specified are
  evaluated together when grouping is established (so you won't get data back
  for each individual column level).

▶ Every column listed in GROUP BY must be a retrieved column or a valid expression (but not an aggregate function). If an expression is used in the SELECT, that same expression must be specified in GROUP BY. Aliases cannot be used.

▶ Most SQL implementations do not allow GROUP BY columns with variable-length datatypes (such as text or memo fields).

▶ Aside from the aggregate calculation statements, every column in your SELECT statement must be present in the GROUP BY clause.

▶ If the grouping column contains a row with a NULL value, NULL will be returned as a group. If there are multiple rows with NULL values, they'll all be grouped together.

▶ The GROUP BY clause must come after any WHERE clause and before any ORDER BY clause.

TIP: **The ALL Clause**
Some SQL implementations (such as Microsoft SQL Server) support an optional ALL clause within GROUP BY. This clause can be used to return all groups, even those that have no matching rows (in which case the aggregate would return NULL). Refer to your DBMS documentation to see if it supports ALL.

CAUTION: **Specifying Columns by Relative Position**
Some SQL implementations allow you to specify GROUP BY columns by the position in the SELECT list. For example, GROUP BY 2,1 can mean *group by the second column selected and then by the first*. Although this shorthand syntax is convenient, it is not supported by all SQL implementations. Its use is also risky in that it is highly susceptible to the introduction of errors when editing SQL statements.

Filtering Groups

In addition to being able to group data using GROUP BY, SQL also allows you to filter which groups to include and which to exclude. For example, you might want a list of all customers who have made at least two orders. To obtain this data, you must filter based on the complete group, not on individual rows.

You've already seen the WHERE clause in action (that was introduced back in Lesson 4, "Filtering Data"). But WHERE does not work here because WHERE filters specific rows, not groups. As a matter of fact, WHERE has no idea what a group is.

So what do you use instead of WHERE? SQL provides yet another clause for this purpose: the HAVING clause. HAVING is very similar to WHERE. In fact, all types of WHERE clauses you've learned about thus far can also be used with HAVING. The only difference is that WHERE filters rows and HAVING filters groups.

> TIP: HAVING **Supports All** WHERE**'s Operators**
> In Lesson 4 and Lesson 5, "Advanced Data Filtering," you learned about WHERE clause conditions (including wildcard conditions and clauses with multiple operators). All the techniques and options that you've learned about WHERE can be applied to HAVING. The syntax is identical; just the keyword is different.

So how do you filter groups? Look at the following example:

Input ▼

```
SELECT cust_id, COUNT(*) AS orders
FROM Orders
GROUP BY cust_id
HAVING COUNT(*) >= 2;
```

Output ▼

```
cust_id    orders
---------- -----------
1000000001 2
```

Analysis ▼

The first three lines of this SELECT statement are similar to the statements seen above. The final line adds a HAVING clause that filters on those groups with a COUNT(*) >= 2—two or more orders.

As you can see, a WHERE clause couldn't work here because the filtering is based on the group aggregate value, not on the values of specific rows.

> NOTE: **The Difference Between** HAVING **and** WHERE
> Here's another way to look it: WHERE filters before data is grouped, and HAVING filters after data is grouped. This is an important distinction; rows that are eliminated by a WHERE clause will not be included in the group. This could change the calculated values, which in turn could affect which groups are filtered based on the use of those values in the HAVING clause.

So is there ever a need to use both WHERE and HAVING clauses in one statement? Actually, yes, there is. Suppose you want to further filter the above statement so that it returns any customers who placed two or more orders in the past 12 months. To do that, you can add a WHERE clause that filters out just the orders placed in the past 12 months. You then add a HAVING clause to filter just the groups with two or more rows in them.

To better demonstrate this, look at the following example, which lists all vendors who have two or more products priced at 4 or more:

Input ▼

```
SELECT vend_id, COUNT(*) AS num_prods
FROM Products
WHERE prod_price >= 4
GROUP BY vend_id
HAVING COUNT(*) >= 2;
```

Output ▼

```
vend_id  num_prods
-------  -----------
BRS01    3
FNG01    2
```

Analysis ▼

This statement warrants an explanation. The first line is a basic SELECT using an aggregate function—much like the examples thus far. The WHERE clause filters all rows with a prod_price of at least 4. Data is then grouped by vend_id, and then a HAVING clause filters just those groups with a count of 2 or more. Without the WHERE clause, an extra row would have been retrieved (vendor DLL01 who sells four products all priced under 4) as seen here:

Input ▼

```
SELECT vend_id, COUNT(*) AS num_prods
FROM Products
GROUP BY vend_id
HAVING COUNT(*) >= 2;
```

Output ▼

```
vend_id  num_prods
-------  -----------
BRS01    3
DLL01    4
FNG01    2
```

NOTE: **Using** HAVING **and** WHERE

HAVING is so similar to WHERE that most DBMSs treat them as the same thing
if no GROUP BY is specified. Nevertheless, you should make that distinction
yourself. Use HAVING only in conjunction with GROUP BY clauses. Use WHERE for
standard row-level filtering.

Grouping and Sorting

It is important to understand that GROUP BY and ORDER BY are very different, even
though they often accomplish the same thing. Table 10.1 summarizes the differences
between them.

TABLE 10.1   ORDER BY Versus GROUP BY

ORDER BY	GROUP BY
Sorts generated output.	Groups rows. The output might not be in group order, however.
Any columns (even columns not selected) may be used.	Only selected columns or expressions columns may be used, and every selected column expression must be used.
Never required.	Required if using columns (or expressions) with aggregate functions.

The first difference listed in Table 10.1 is extremely important. More often than not,
you will find that data grouped using GROUP BY will indeed be output in group order.
But that is not always the case, and it is not actually required by the SQL specifica-
tions. Furthermore, even if your particular DBMS does, in fact, always sort the data
by the specified GROUP BY clause, you might actually want it sorted differently. Just
because you group data one way (to obtain group-specific aggregate values) does not
mean that you want the output sorted that same way. You should always provide an
explicit ORDER BY clause as well, even if it is identical to the GROUP BY clause.

TIP: **Don't Forget** ORDER BY

As a rule, anytime you use a GROUP BY clause, you should also specify an
ORDER BY clause. That is the only way to ensure that data will be sorted
properly. Never rely on GROUP BY to sort your data.

To demonstrate the use of both GROUP BY and ORDER BY, let's look at an example.
The following SELECT statement is similar to the ones seen previously. It retrieves

the order number and number of items ordered for all orders containing three or more items:

Input ▼

```
SELECT order_num, COUNT(*) AS items
FROM OrderItems
GROUP BY order_num
HAVING COUNT(*) >= 3;
```

Output ▼

```
order_num  items
---------  -----
20006      3
20007      5
20008      5
20009      3
```

To sort the output by number of items ordered, all you need to do is add an ORDER BY clause, as follows:

Input ▼

```
SELECT order_num, COUNT(*) AS items
FROM OrderItems
GROUP BY order_num
HAVING COUNT(*) >= 3
ORDER BY items, order_num;
```

Output ▼

```
order_num  items
---------  -----
20006      3
20009      3
20007      5
20008      5
```

Analysis ▼

In this example, the GROUP BY clause is used to group the data by order number (the order_num column) so that the COUNT(*) function can return the number of items in each order. The HAVING clause filters the data so that only orders with three or more items are returned. Finally, the output is sorted using the ORDER BY clause.

SELECT **Clause Ordering**

This is probably a good time to review the order in which SELECT statement clauses are to be specified. Table 10.2 lists all the clauses we have learned thus far, in the order they must be used.

TABLE 10.2 SELECT Clauses and Their Sequence

Clause	Description	Required
SELECT	Columns or expressions to be returned	Yes
FROM	Table to retrieve data from	Only if selecting data from a table
WHERE	Row-level filtering	No
GROUP BY	Group specification	Only if calculating aggregates by group
HAVING	Group-level filtering	No
ORDER BY	Output sort order	No

Summary

In Lesson 9, "Summarizing Data," you learned how to use the SQL aggregate functions to perform summary calculations on your data. In this lesson, you learned how to use the GROUP BY clause to perform these calculations on groups of data, returning results for each group. You saw how to use the HAVING clause to filter specific groups. You also learned the difference between ORDER BY and GROUP BY and between WHERE and HAVING.

Challenges

1. The OrderItems table contains the individual items for each order. Write a SQL statement that returns the number of lines (as order_lines) for each order number (order_num) and sort the results by order_lines.

2. Write a SQL statement that returns a field named cheapest_item, which contains the lowest-cost item for each vendor (using prod_price in the Products table), and sort the results from lowest to highest cost.

3. It's important to identify the best customers, so write a SQL statement to return the order number (order_num in the OrderItems table) for all orders of at least 100 items.

4. Another way to determine the best customers is by how much they have spent. Write a SQL statement to return the order number (order_num in the OrderItems table) for all orders with a total price of at least 1000. Hint: for this one you'll need to calculate and sum the total (item_price multiplied by quantity). Sort the results by order number.

5. What is wrong with the following SQL statement? (Try to figure it out without running it.)

```
SELECT order_num, COUNT(*) AS items
FROM OrderItems
GROUP BY items
HAVING COUNT(*) >= 3
ORDER BY items, order_num;
```

LESSON 11

Working with Subqueries

In this lesson, you'll learn what subqueries are and how to use them.

Understanding Subqueries

SELECT statements are SQL queries. All the SELECT statements we have seen thus far are simple queries—single statements retrieving data from individual database tables.

> NEW TERM: **Query**
>
> Any SQL statement. However, the term is usually used to refer to SELECT statements.

SQL also enables you to create subqueries—queries that are embedded into other queries. Why would you want to do this? The best way to understand this concept is to look at a couple of examples.

Filtering by Subquery

The database tables used in all the lessons in this book are relational tables. (See Appendix A, "Sample Table Scripts," for a description of each of the tables and their relationships.) Orders are stored in two tables. The Orders table stores a single row for each order containing order number, customer ID, and order date. The individual order items are stored in the related OrderItems table. The Orders table does not store customer information. It only stores a customer ID. The actual customer information is stored in the Customers table.

Now suppose you wanted a list of all the customers who ordered item RGAN01. What would you have to do to retrieve this information? Here are the steps:

1. Retrieve the order numbers of all orders containing item RGAN01.

2. Retrieve the customer ID of all the customers who have orders listed in the order numbers returned in the previous step.

3. Retrieve the customer information for all the customer IDs returned in the previous step.

Each of these steps can be executed as a separate query. By doing so, you use the results returned by one SELECT statement to populate the WHERE clause of the next SELECT statement.

You can also use subqueries to combine all three queries into one single statement.

The first SELECT statement should be self-explanatory by now. It retrieves the order_num column for all order items with a prod_id of RGAN01. The output lists the two orders containing this item:

Input ▼

```
SELECT order_num
FROM OrderItems
WHERE prod_id = 'RGAN01';
```

Output ▼

```
order_num
-----------
20007
20008
```

Now that we know which orders contain the desired item, the next step is to retrieve the customer IDs associated with those order number, 20007 and 20008. Using the IN clause described in Lesson 5, "Advanced Data Filtering," you can create a SELECT statement as follows:

Input ▼

```
SELECT cust_id
FROM Orders
WHERE order_num IN (20007,20008);
```

Output ▼

```
cust_id
----------
1000000004
1000000005
```

Now, combine the two queries by turning the first (the one that returned the order numbers) into a subquery. Look at the following SELECT statement:

Input ▼

```
SELECT cust_id
FROM Orders
WHERE order_num IN (SELECT order_num
                    FROM OrderItems
                    WHERE prod_id = 'RGAN01');
```

Output ▼

```
cust_id
----------
1000000004
1000000005
```

Analysis ▼

Subqueries are always processed starting with the innermost SELECT statement and working outward. When the preceding SELECT statement is processed, the DBMS actually performs two operations.

It first runs the following subquery:

```
SELECT order_num FROM orderitems WHERE prod_id='RGAN01'
```

That query returns the two order numbers 20007 and 20008. Those two values are then passed to the WHERE clause of the outer query in the comma-delimited format required by the IN operator. The outer query now becomes

```
SELECT cust_id FROM orders WHERE order_num IN (20007,20008)
```

As you can see, the output is correct and exactly the same as the output returned by the hard-coded WHERE clause above.

> TIP: **Formatting Your SQL**
>
> SELECT statements containing subqueries can be difficult to read and debug, especially as they grow in complexity. Breaking up the queries over multiple lines and indenting the lines appropriately as shown here can greatly simplify working with subqueries.
>
> Incidentally, this is where color coding also becomes invaluable, and the better DBMS clients do indeed color code SQL for just this reason. And this is also why the SQL statements in this book have been printed in color for you; it makes reading them, isolating their sections, and troubleshooting them so much easier.

You now have the IDs of all the customers who ordered item RGAN01. The next step is to retrieve the customer information for each of those customer IDs. Here is the SQL statement to retrieve the two columns:

Input ▼

```
SELECT cust_name, cust_contact
FROM Customers
WHERE cust_id IN (1000000004,1000000005);
```

Instead of hard-coding those customer IDs, you can turn this WHERE clause into yet another subquery:

Input ▼

```
SELECT cust_name, cust_contact
FROM Customers
WHERE cust_id IN (SELECT cust_id
                  FROM Orders
                  WHERE order_num IN (SELECT order_num
                                      FROM OrderItems
                                      WHERE prod_id = 'RGAN01'));
```

Output ▼

cust_name	cust_contact
Fun4All	Denise L. Stephens
The Toy Store	Kim Howard

Analysis ▼

To execute the above SELECT statement, the DBMS had to actually perform three SELECT statements. The innermost subquery returned a list of order numbers that were then used as the WHERE clause for the subquery above it. That subquery returned a list of customer IDs that were used as the WHERE clause for the top-level query. The top-level query actually returned the desired data.

As you can see, using subqueries in a WHERE clause enables you to write extremely powerful and flexible SQL statements. There is no limit imposed on the number of subqueries that can be nested, although in practice you will find that performance will tell you when you are nesting too deeply.

> CAUTION: **Single Column Only**
> Subquery SELECT statements can only retrieve a single column. Attempting to retrieve multiple columns will return an error.

> CAUTION: **Subqueries and Performance**
>
> The code shown here works, and it achieves the desired result. However, using subqueries is not always the most efficient way to perform this type of data retrieval. More on this in Lesson 12, "Joining Tables," where you will revisit this same example.

Using Subqueries as Calculated Fields

Another way to use subqueries is in creating calculated fields. Suppose you wanted to display the total number of orders placed by every customer in your Customers table. Orders are stored in the Orders table along with the appropriate customer ID.

To perform this operation, follow these steps:

1. Retrieve the list of customers from the Customers table.

2. For each customer retrieved, count the number of associated orders in the Orders table.

As you learned in the previous two lessons, you can use SELECT COUNT(*) to count rows in a table, and by providing a WHERE clause to filter a specific customer ID, you can count just that customer's orders. For example, the following code counts the number of orders placed by customer 1000000001:

Input ▼

```
SELECT COUNT(*) AS orders
FROM Orders
WHERE cust_id = 1000000001;
```

To perform that COUNT(*) calculation for each customer, use COUNT* as a subquery. Look at the following code:

Input ▼

```
SELECT cust_name,
       cust_state,
       (SELECT COUNT(*)
        FROM Orders
        WHERE Orders.cust_id = Customers.cust_id) AS orders
FROM Customers
ORDER BY cust_name;
```

Output ▼

cust_name	cust_state	orders
Fun4All	IN	1
Fun4All	AZ	1
Kids Place	OH	0
The Toy Store	IL	1
Village Toys	MI	2

Analysis ▼

This SELECT statement returns three columns for every customer in the Customers table: cust_name, cust_state, and orders. Orders is a calculated field that is set by a subquery that is provided in parentheses. That subquery is executed once for every customer retrieved. In the example above, the subquery is executed five times because five customers were retrieved.

The WHERE clause in the subquery is a little different from the WHERE clauses used previously because it uses fully qualified column names; instead of just a column name (cust_id), it specifies the table and the column name (as Orders.cust_id and Customers.cust_id). The following WHERE clause tells SQL to compare the cust_id in the Orders table to the one currently being retrieved from the Customers table:

```
WHERE Orders.cust_id = Customers.cust_id
```

This syntax—the table name and the column name separated by a period—must be used whenever there is possible ambiguity about column names. In this example, there are two cust_id columns, one in Customers and one in Orders. Without fully qualifying the column names, the DBMS assumes you are comparing the cust_id in the Orders table to itself. Because

```
SELECT COUNT(*) FROM Orders WHERE cust_id = cust_id
```

will always return the total number of orders in the Orders table, the results will not be what you expected:

Input ▼

```
SELECT cust_name,
       cust_state,
       (SELECT COUNT(*)
        FROM Orders
        WHERE cust_id = cust_id) AS orders
FROM Customers
ORDER BY cust_name;
```

Output ▼

cust_name	cust_state	orders
Fun4All	IN	5
Fun4All	AZ	5
Kids Place	OH	5
The Toy Store	IL	5
Village Toys	MI	5

Although subqueries are extremely useful in constructing this type of SELECT statement, care must be taken to properly qualify ambiguous column names.

CAUTION: **Fully Qualified Column Names**

You just saw a very important reason to use fully qualified column names. Without the extra specificity, the wrong results were returned because the DBMS misunderstood what you intended. Sometimes the ambiguity caused by the presence of conflicting column names will actually cause the DBMS to throw an error. For example, this might occur if your WHERE or ORDER BY clause specified a column name that was present in multiple tables. A good rule is that if you are ever working with more than one table in a SELECT statement, then use fully qualified column names to avoid any and all ambiguity.

TIP: **Subqueries May Not Always Be the Best Option**

As explained earlier in this lesson, although the sample code shown here works, it is often not the most efficient way to perform this type of data retrieval. You will revisit this example when you learn about JOINs in the next two lessons.

Summary

In this lesson, you learned what subqueries are and how to use them. The most common uses for subqueries are in WHERE clause IN operators and for populating calculated columns. You saw examples of both of these types of operations.

Challenges

1. Using a subquery, return a list of customers who bought items priced 10 or more. You'll want to use the OrderItems table to find the matching order numbers (order_num) and then the Orders table to retrieve the customer ID (cust_id) for those matched orders.

2. You need to know the dates when product BR01 was ordered. Write a SQL statement that uses a subquery to determine which orders (in OrderItems) purchased items with a prod_id of BR01 and then returns customer ID (cust_id) and order date (order_date) for each from the Orders table. Sort the results by order date.

3. Now let's make it a bit more challenging. Update the previous challenge to return the customer email (cust_email in the Customers table) for any customers who purchased items with a prod_id of BR01. Hint: this involves the SELECT statement, the innermost one returning order_num from OrderItems, and the middle one returning cust_id from Customers.

4. We need a list of customer IDs with the total amount they have ordered. Write a SQL statement to return customer ID (cust_id in the Orders table) and total_ordered using a subquery to return the total of orders for each customer. Sort the results by amount spent from greatest to the least. Hint: you've used the SUM() to calculate order totals previously.

5. One more. Write a SQL statement that retrieves all product names (prod_name) from the Products table, along with a calculated column named quant_sold containing the total number of this item sold (retrieved using a subquery and a SUM(quantity) on the OrderItems table).

Joining Tables

In this lesson, you'll learn what joins are, why they are used, and how to create SELECT *statements using them.*

Understanding Joins

One of SQL's most powerful features is the capability to join tables on-the-fly within data retrieval queries. Joins are one of the most important operations that you can perform using SQL SELECT, and a good understanding of joins and join syntax is an extremely important part of learning SQL.

Before you can effectively use joins, you must understand relational tables and the basics of relational database design. What follows is by no means complete coverage of the subject, but it should be enough to get you up and running.

Understanding Relational Tables

The best way to understand relational tables is to look at a real-world example, one based on the data you've used in the lessons thus far.

Suppose you had a database table containing a product list, with each product in its own row. The kind of information you would store with each product would include a description and price, along with vendor information about the company that creates the product.

Now suppose that you had multiple products created by the same vendor. Where would you store the vendor information (things like vendor name, address, and contact information)? You wouldn't want to store that data along with the products for several reasons:

▶ Because the vendor information is the same for each product that vendor produces, repeating the information for each product is a waste of time and storage space.

▶ If vendor information changes (for example, if the vendor moves or the contact info changes), you would need to update every occurrence of the vendor information.

▶ When data is repeated (that is, the vendor information is used with each product), there is a high likelihood that the data will not be entered identically each time. Inconsistent data is extremely difficult to use in reporting.

The key here is that having multiple occurrences of the same data is never a good thing, and that principle is the basis for relational database design. Relational tables are designed so that information is split into multiple tables, one for each data type. The tables are related to each other through common values (and thus the *relational* in relational design).

In our example, you can create two tables—one for vendor information and one for product information. The Vendors table contains all the vendor information, one table row per vendor, along with a unique identifier for each vendor. This value, called a *primary key*, can be a vendor ID or any other unique value.

The Products table stores only product information and no vendor-specific information other than the vendor ID (the Vendors table's primary key). This key relates the Vendors table to the Products table, and using this vendor ID enables you to use the Vendors table to find the details about the appropriate vendor.

What does this do for you? Well, consider the following:

▶ Vendor information is never repeated, and so time and space are not wasted.

▶ If vendor information changes, you can update a single record, the one in the Vendors table. Data in related tables does not change.

▶ Because no data is repeated, the data used is obviously consistent, making data reporting and manipulation much simpler.

The bottom line is that relational data can be stored efficiently and manipulated easily. Because of this, relational databases *scale* far better than nonrelational databases.

NEW TERM: **Scale**
Able to handle an increasing load without failing. A well-designed database or application is said to *scale well*.

Why Use Joins?

As just explained, breaking data into multiple tables enables more efficient storage, easier manipulation, and greater scalability. But these benefits come with a price.

If data is stored in multiple tables, how can you retrieve that data with a single SELECT statement?

The answer is to use a join. Simply put, a join is a mechanism used to associate, or join, tables within a SELECT statement (and thus the name *join*). By using a special syntax, you can join multiple tables so that a single set of output is returned, and the join associates the correct rows in each table on the fly.

> **NOTE: Using Interactive DBMS Tools**
>
> Understand that a join is not a physical entity; in other words, it does not exist in the actual database tables. A join is created by the DBMS as needed, and it persists for the duration of the query execution.
>
> Many DBMSs provide graphical interfaces that can be used to define table relationships interactively. These tools can be invaluable in helping to maintain referential integrity. When you are using relational tables, it is important that only valid data is inserted into relational columns. Going back to the example, if an invalid vendor ID is stored in the Products table, those products would be inaccessible because they would not be related to any vendor. To prevent this from occurring, you can instruct the database to only allow valid values (ones present in the Vendors table) in the vendor ID column in the Products table. Referential integrity means that the DBMS enforces data integrity rules. And these rules are often managed through DBMS provided interfaces.

Creating a Join

Creating a join is very simple. You must specify all the tables to be included and how they are related to each other. Look at the following example:

Input ▼

```
SELECT vend_name, prod_name, prod_price
FROM Vendors, Products
WHERE Vendors.vend_id = Products.vend_id;
```

Output ▼

```
vend_name              prod_name              prod_price
-------------------    --------------------   ----------
Doll House Inc.        Fish bean bag toy      3.4900
Doll House Inc.        Bird bean bag toy      3.4900
Doll House Inc.        Rabbit bean bag toy    3.4900
Bears R Us             8 inch teddy bear      5.9900
Bears R Us             12 inch teddy bear     8.9900
Bears R Us             18 inch teddy bear     11.9900
Doll House Inc.        Raggedy Ann            4.9900
Fun and Games          King doll              9.4900
Fun and Games          Queen doll             9.4900
```

Analysis ▼

Let's take a look at the preceding code. The SELECT statement starts in the same way as all the statements you've looked at thus far, by specifying the columns to be retrieved. The big difference here is that two of the specified columns (prod_name and prod_price) are in one table, whereas the other (vend_name) is in another table.

Now look at the FROM clause. Unlike all the prior SELECT statements, this one has two tables listed in the FROM clause, Vendors and Products. These are the names of the two tables that are being joined in this SELECT statement. The tables are correctly joined with a WHERE clause that instructs the DBMS to match vend_id in the Vendors table with vend_id in the Products table.

You'll notice that the columns are specified as Vendors.vend_id and Products.vend_id. This fully qualified column name is required here because if you just specified vend_id, the DBMS cannot tell which vend_id columns you are referring to. (There are two of them, one in each table.) As you can see in the preceding output, a single SELECT statement returns data from two different tables.

CAUTION: **Fully Qualifying Column Names**

As noted in the previous lesson, you must use the fully qualified column name (table and column separated by a period) whenever there is a possible ambiguity about which column you are referring to. Most DBMSs will return an error message if you refer to an ambiguous column name without fully qualifying it with a table name.

The Importance of the WHERE Clause

It might seem strange to use a WHERE clause to set the join relationship, but actually, there is a very good reason for this. Remember, when tables are joined in a SELECT statement, that relationship is constructed on the fly. There is nothing in the database table definitions that can instruct the DBMS how to join the tables. You have to do that yourself. When you join two tables, what you are actually doing is pairing every row in the first table with every row in the second table. The WHERE clause acts as a filter to only include rows that match the specified filter condition—the join condition, in this case. Without the WHERE clause, every row in the first table will be paired with every row in the second table, regardless of whether they logically go together or not.

NEW TERM: **Cartesian Product**

The results returned by a table relationship without a join condition. The number of rows retrieved will be the number of rows in the first table multiplied by the number of rows in the second table.

To understand this, look at the following SELECT statement and output:

Input ▼

```
SELECT vend_name, prod_name, prod_price
FROM Vendors, Products;
```

Output ▼

vend_name	prod_name	prod_price
Bears R Us	8 inch teddy bear	5.99
Bears R Us	12 inch teddy bear	8.99
Bears R Us	18 inch teddy bear	11.99
Bears R Us	Fish bean bag toy	3.49
Bears R Us	Bird bean bag toy	3.49
Bears R Us	Rabbit bean bag toy	3.49
Bears R Us	Raggedy Ann	4.99
Bears R Us	King doll	9.49
Bears R Us	Queen doll	9.49
Bear Emporium	8 inch teddy bear	5.99
Bear Emporium	12 inch teddy bear	8.99
Bear Emporium	18 inch teddy bear	11.99
Bear Emporium	Fish bean bag toy	3.49
Bear Emporium	Bird bean bag toy	3.49
Bear Emporium	Rabbit bean bag toy	3.49
Bear Emporium	Raggedy Ann	4.99
Bear Emporium	King doll	9.49
Bear Emporium	Queen doll	9.49
Doll House Inc.	8 inch teddy bear	5.99
Doll House Inc.	12 inch teddy bear	8.99
Doll House Inc.	18 inch teddy bear	11.99
Doll House Inc.	Fish bean bag toy	3.49
Doll House Inc.	Bird bean bag toy	3.49
Doll House Inc.	Rabbit bean bag toy	3.49
Doll House Inc.	Raggedy Ann	4.99
Doll House Inc.	King doll	9.49
Doll House Inc.	Queen doll	9.49
Furball Inc.	8 inch teddy bear	5.99
Furball Inc.	12 inch teddy bear	8.99
Furball Inc.	18 inch teddy bear	11.99
Furball Inc.	Fish bean bag toy	3.49
Furball Inc.	Bird bean bag toy	3.49
Furball Inc.	Rabbit bean bag toy	3.49
Furball Inc.	Raggedy Ann	4.99
Furball Inc.	King doll	9.49
Furball Inc.	Queen doll	9.49
Fun and Games	8 inch teddy bear	5.99
Fun and Games	12 inch teddy bear	8.99
Fun and Games	18 inch teddy bear	11.99
Fun and Games	Fish bean bag toy	3.49

Fun and Games	Bird bean bag toy	3.49
Fun and Games	Rabbit bean bag toy	3.49
Fun and Games	Raggedy Ann	4.99
Fun and Games	King doll	9.49
Fun and Games	Queen doll	9.49
Jouets et ours	8 inch teddy bear	5.99
Jouets et ours	12 inch teddy bear	8.99
Jouets et ours	18 inch teddy bear	11.99
Jouets et ours	Fish bean bag toy	3.49
Jouets et ours	Bird bean bag toy	3.49
Jouets et ours	Rabbit bean bag toy	3.49
Jouets et ours	Raggedy Ann	4.99
Jouets et ours	King doll	9.49
Jouets et ours	Queen doll	9.49

Analysis ▼

As you can see in the preceding output, the Cartesian product is seldom what you
want. The data returned here has matched every product with every vendor, including
products with the incorrect vendor (and even vendors with no products at all).

CAUTION: **Don't Forget the WHERE Clause**

Make sure all your joins have WHERE clauses; otherwise, the DBMS will return far
more data than you want. Similarly, make sure your WHERE clauses are correct.
An incorrect filter condition will cause the DBMS to return incorrect data.

TIP: **Cross Joins**

Sometimes you'll hear the type of join that returns a Cartesian Product referred
to as a *cross join*.

Inner Joins

The join you have been using so far is called an *equijoin*—a join based on the testing
of equality between two tables. This kind of join is also called an *inner join*. In fact,
you may use a slightly different syntax for these joins, specifying the type of join
explicitly. The following SELECT statement returns the exact same data as an earlier
example:

Input ▼

```
SELECT vend_name, prod_name, prod_price
FROM Vendors
INNER JOIN Products ON Vendors.vend_id = Products.vend_id;
```

Analysis ▼

The SELECT in the statement is the same as the preceding SELECT statement, but the FROM clause is different. Here the relationship between the two tables is part of the FROM clause specified as INNER JOIN. In this syntax, the join condition is specified using the special ON clause instead of a WHERE clause. The actual condition passed to ON is the same as would be passed to WHERE.

Refer to your DBMS documentation to see which syntax is preferred.

> NOTE: **The "Right" Syntax**
>
> Per the ANSI SQL specification, use of the INNER JOIN syntax is preferred over the simple equijoins syntax used previously. Indeed, SQL purists tend to look upon the simple syntax with disdain. That being said, DBMSs do indeed support both the simpler and the standard formats, so my recommendation is that you take the time to understand both formats but use whichever you feel more comfortable with.

Joining Multiple Tables

SQL imposes no limit to the number of tables that may be joined in a SELECT statement. The basic rules for creating the join remain the same. First, list all the tables, and then define the relationship between each. Here is an example:

Input ▼

```
SELECT prod_name, vend_name, prod_price, quantity
FROM OrderItems, Products, Vendors
WHERE Products.vend_id = Vendors.vend_id
 AND OrderItems.prod_id = Products.prod_id
 AND order_num = 20007;
```

Output ▼

prod_name	vend_name	prod_price	quantity
18 inch teddy bear	Bears R Us	11.9900	50
Fish bean bag toy	Doll House Inc.	3.4900	100
Bird bean bag toy	Doll House Inc.	3.4900	100
Rabbit bean bag toy	Doll House Inc.	3.4900	100
Raggedy Ann	Doll House Inc.	4.9900	50

Analysis ▼

This example displays the items in order number 20007. Order items are stored in
the OrderItems table. Each product is stored by its product ID, which refers to a
product in the Products table. The products are linked to the appropriate vendor in
the Vendors table by the vendor ID, which is stored with each product record. The
FROM clause here lists the three tables, and the WHERE clause defines both of those join
conditions. An additional WHERE condition is then used to filter just the items for order
20007.

> CAUTION: **Performance Considerations**
> DBMSs process joins at runtime relating each table as specified. This
> process can become very resource intensive, so be careful not to join tables
> unnecessarily. The more tables you join, the more performance will degrade.

> CAUTION: **Maximum Number of Tables in a Join**
> While it is true that SQL itself has no maximum number of tables per join
> restriction, many DBMSs do indeed have restrictions. Refer to your DBMS
> documentation to determine what restrictions there are, if any.

Now would be a good time to revisit the following example from Lesson 11,
"Working with Subqueries." As you will recall, this SELECT statement returns a list of
customers who ordered product RGAN01:

Input ▼

```
SELECT cust_name, cust_contact
FROM Customers
WHERE cust_id IN (SELECT cust_id
                  FROM Orders
                  WHERE order_num IN (SELECT order_num
                                      FROM OrderItems
                                      WHERE prod_id = 'RGAN01'));
```

As mentioned in Lesson 11, subqueries are not always the most efficient way to perform
complex SELECT operations, and so as promised, here is the same query using joins:

Input ▼

```
SELECT cust_name, cust_contact
FROM Customers, Orders, OrderItems
WHERE Customers.cust_id = Orders.cust_id
 AND OrderItems.order_num = Orders.order_num
 AND prod_id = 'RGAN01';
```

Output ▼

```
cust_name                          cust_contact
---------------------------        --------------------
Fun4All                            Denise L. Stephens
The Toy Store                      Kim Howard
```

Analysis ▼

As explained in Lesson 11, returning the data needed in this query requires the use of three tables. But instead of using them within nested subqueries, here two joins are used to connect the tables. There are three WHERE clause conditions here. The first two connect the tables in the join, and the last one filters the data for product RGAN01.

TIP: **It Pays to Experiment**

As you can see, there is often more than one way to perform any given SQL operation. And there is rarely a definitive right or wrong way. Performance can be affected by the type of operation, the DBMS being used, the amount of data in the tables, whether or not indexes and keys are present, and a whole slew of other criteria. Therefore, it is often worth experimenting with different selection mechanisms to find the one that works best for you.

NOTE: **Joined Column Names**

In all of the examples presented here, the columns being joined are named the same (cust_id in both Customers and Orders, for example). Having identically named columns is not a requirement, and you'll often encounter databases that use different naming conventions. I created the tables this way to make the examples simpler and clearer.

Summary

Joins are one of the most important and powerful features in SQL, and using them effectively requires a basic understanding of relational database design. In this lesson, you learned some of the basics of relational database design as an introduction to learning about joins. You also learned how to create an equijoin (also known as an inner join), which is the most commonly used form of join. In the next lesson, you'll learn how to create other types of joins.

Challenges

1. Write a SQL statement to return customer name (cust_name) from the Customers table and related order numbers (order_num) from the Orders table, sorting the result by customer name and then by order number. Actually, try this one twice—once using simple equijoin syntax and once using an INNER JOIN.

2. Let's make the previous challenge more useful. In addition to returning the customer name and order number, add a third column named OrderTotal containing the total price of each order. There are two ways to do this: you can create the OrderTotal column using a subquery on the OrderItems table, or you can join the OrderItems table to the existing tables and use an aggregate function. Here's a hint: watch out for where you need to use fully qualified column names.

3. Let's revisit Challenge 2 from Lesson 11. Write a SQL statement that retrieves the dates when product BR01 was ordered, but this time use a join and simple equijoin syntax. The output should be identical to the one from Lesson 11.

4. That was fun; let's try it again. Re-create the SQL you wrote for Lesson 11 Challenge 3, but this time using ANSI INNER JOIN syntax. The code you wrote there employed two nested subqueries. To re-create it, you'll need two INNER JOIN statements, each formatted like the INNER JOIN example earlier in this lesson. And don't forget the WHERE clause to filter by prod_id.

5. One more, and to make things more fun, we'll mix joins, aggregate functions, and grouping too. Ready? Back in Lesson 10 I issued you a challenge to find all order numbers with a value of 1000 or more. Those results are useful, but what would be even more useful is the names of the customers who placed orders of at least that amount. So, write a SQL statement that uses joins to return customer name (cust_name) from the Customers table and the total price of all orders from the OrderItems table. Here's a hint: to join those tables, you'll also need to include the Orders table (because Customers is not related directly to OrderItems, Customers is related to Orders, and Orders is related to OrderItems). Don't forget GROUP BY and HAVING, and sort the results by customer name. You can use simple equijoin or ANSI INNER JOIN syntax for this one. Or, if you are feeling brave, try writing it both ways.

LESSON 13

Creating Advanced Joins

In this lesson, you'll learn all about additional join types—what they are and how to use them. You'll also learn how to use table aliases and how to use aggregate functions with joined tables.

Using Table Aliases

Before we look at additional types of joins, we need to revisit aliases. Back in Lesson 7, "Creating Calculated Fields," you learned how to use aliases to refer to retrieved table columns. The syntax to alias a column (in SQL Server) looks like this:

Input ▼

```
SELECT RTRIM(vend_name) + ' (' + RTRIM(vend_country) + ')'
       AS vend_title
FROM Vendors
ORDER BY vend_name;
```

In addition to using aliases for column names and calculated fields, SQL also enables you to alias table names. There are two primary reasons to do this:

▶ To shorten the SQL syntax

▶ To enable multiple uses of the same table within a single SELECT statement

Take a look at the following SELECT statement. It is basically the same statement as an example used in the previous lesson, but it has been modified to use aliases:

Input ▼

```
SELECT cust_name, cust_contact
FROM Customers AS C, Orders AS O, OrderItems AS OI
WHERE C.cust_id = O.cust_id
 AND OI.order_num = O.order_num
 AND prod_id = 'RGAN01';
```

Analysis ▼

You'll notice that the three tables in the FROM clauses all have aliases. Customers AS C establishes C as an alias for Customers, and so on. This approach enables you to use the abbreviated C instead of the full text Customers. In this example, the table aliases were used only in the WHERE clause, but aliases are not limited to just WHERE. You can use aliases in the SELECT list, the ORDER BY clause, and in any other part of the statement as well.

> CAUTION: **No AS in Oracle**
>
> Oracle does not support the AS keyword when aliasing tables. To use aliases in Oracle, simply specify the alias without AS (so Customers C instead of Customers AS C).

It is also worth noting that table aliases are only used during query execution. Unlike column aliases, table aliases are never returned to the client.

Using Different Join Types

Thus far you have used only simple joins known as inner joins or *equijoins*. You'll now take a look at three additional join types: the self join, the natural join, and the outer join.

Self Joins

As mentioned earlier, one of the primary reasons to use table aliases is to be able to refer to the same table more than once in a single SELECT statement. An example will demonstrate this.

Suppose you wanted to send a mailing to all the customer contacts who work for the same company for which Jim Jones works. This query requires that you first find out which company Jim Jones works for and next which customers work for that company. The following is one way to approach this problem:

Input ▼

```
SELECT cust_id, cust_name, cust_contact
FROM Customers
WHERE cust_name = (SELECT cust_name
                   FROM Customers
                   WHERE cust_contact = 'Jim Jones');
```

Output ▼

cust_id	cust_name	cust_contact
1000000003	Fun4All	Jim Jones
1000000004	Fun4All	Denise L. Stephens

Analysis ▼

This first solution uses subqueries. The inner SELECT statement does a simple retrieval to return the cust_name of the company that Jim Jones works for. That name is the one used in the WHERE clause of the outer query so that all employees who work for that company are retrieved. (You learned all about subqueries in Lesson 11, "Working with Subqueries." Refer to that lesson for more information.)

Now look at the same query using a join:

Input ▼

```
SELECT c1.cust_id, c1.cust_name, c1.cust_contact
FROM Customers AS c1, Customers AS c2
WHERE c1.cust_name = c2.cust_name
 AND c2.cust_contact = 'Jim Jones';
```

Output ▼

cust_id	cust_name	cust_contact
1000000003	Fun4All	Jim Jones
1000000004	Fun4All	Denise L. Stephens

> TIP: **No AS in Oracle**
> Oracle users, remember to drop the AS.

Analysis ▼

The two tables needed in this query are actually the same table, and so the Customers table appears in the FROM clause twice. Although this is perfectly legal, any references to table Customers would be ambiguous because the DBMS does not know which Customers table you are referring to.

To resolve this problem, table aliases are used. The first occurrence of Customers has an alias of c1, and the second has an alias of c2. Now those aliases can be used as table names. The SELECT statement, for example, uses the c1 prefix to explicitly state the full name of the desired columns. If it did not, the DBMS would return an error because there are two of each column named `cust_id`, `cust_name`, and `cust_contact`. It cannot know which one you want. (Even though they are the same.) The WHERE clause first joins the tables and then filters the data by `cust_contact` in the second table to return only the wanted data.

TIP: **Self Joins Instead of Subqueries**

Self joins are often used to replace statements using subqueries that retrieve data from the same table as the outer statement. Although the end result is the same, many DBMSs process joins far more quickly than they do subqueries. It is usually worth experimenting with both to determine which performs better.

Natural Joins ▼

Whenever tables are joined, at least one column will appear in more than one table (the columns being used to create the join). Standard joins (the inner joins that you learned about in the last lesson) return all data, even multiple occurrences of the same column. A natural join simply eliminates those multiple occurrences so that only one of each column is returned.

How does it do this? The answer is it doesn't—you do it. A natural join is a join in which you select only columns that are unique. This is typically done using a wildcard (SELECT *) for one table and explicit subsets of the columns for all other tables. The following is an example:

Input ▼

```
SELECT C.*, O.order_num, O.order_date,
       OI.prod_id, OI.quantity, OI.item_price
FROM Customers AS C, Orders AS O,
     OrderItems AS OI
WHERE C.cust_id = O.cust_id
 AND OI.order_num = O.order_num
 AND prod_id = 'RGAN01';
```

TIP: **No AS in Oracle**

Oracle users, remember to drop the AS.

Analysis ▼

In this example, a wildcard is used for the first table only. All other columns are explicitly listed so that no duplicate columns are retrieved.

The truth is, every inner join you have created thus far is actually a natural join, and you will probably never need an inner join that is not a natural join.

Outer Joins

Most joins relate rows in one table with rows in another. But occasionally, you want to include rows that have no related rows. For example, you might use joins to accomplish the following tasks:

▶ Count how many orders were placed by each customer, including customers that have yet to place an order.

▶ List all products with order quantities, including products not ordered by anyone.

▶ Calculate average sale sizes, taking into account customers that have not yet placed an order.

In each of these examples, the join includes table rows that have no associated rows in the related table. This type of join is called an outer join.

> CAUTION: **Syntax Differences**
>
> It is important to note that the syntax used to create an outer join can vary slightly among different SQL implementations. The various forms of syntax described in the following section cover most implementations, but refer to your DBMS documentation to verify its syntax before proceeding.

The following SELECT statement is a simple inner join. It retrieves a list of all customers and their orders:

Input ▼

```
SELECT Customers.cust_id, Orders.order_num
FROM Customers
 INNER JOIN Orders ON Customers.cust_id = Orders.cust_id;
```

Outer join syntax is similar. To retrieve a list of all customers including those who have placed no orders, you can do the following:

Input ▼

```
SELECT Customers.cust_id, Orders.order_num
FROM Customers
 LEFT OUTER JOIN Orders ON Customers.cust_id = Orders.cust_id;
```

Output ▼

```
cust_id      order_num
----------   ---------
1000000001   20005
1000000001   20009
1000000002   NULL
1000000003   20006
1000000004   20007
1000000005   20008
```

Analysis ▼

Like the inner join seen in the last lesson, this SELECT statement uses the keywords
OUTER JOIN to specify the join type (instead of specifying it in the WHERE clause). But
unlike inner joins, which relate rows in both tables, outer joins also include rows with
no related rows. When using OUTER JOIN syntax, you must use the RIGHT or LEFT
keywords to specify the table from which to include all rows (RIGHT for the one on
the right of OUTER JOIN and LEFT for the one on the left). The previous example uses
LEFT OUTER JOIN to select all the rows from the table on the left in the FROM clause
(the Customers table). To select all the rows from the table on the right, you use a
RIGHT OUTER JOIN as seen in this next example:

Input ▼

```
SELECT Customers.cust_id, Orders.order_num
FROM Customers
 RIGHT OUTER JOIN Orders ON Customers.cust_id = Orders.cust_id;
```

CAUTION: **SQLite Outer Joins**

SQLite supports LEFT OUTER JOIN, but not RIGHT OUTER JOIN. Fortunately, if
you do need RIGHT OUTER JOIN functionality in SQLite, there is a very simple
solution as will be explained in the next tip.

TIP: **Outer Join Types**

Remember that there are always two basic forms of outer joins—the left outer
join and the right outer join. The only difference between them is the order of
the tables that they are relating. In other words, a left outer join can be turned
into a right outer join simply by reversing the order of the tables in the FROM or
WHERE clause. As such, the two types of outer join can be used interchangeably,
and the decision about which one is used is based purely on convenience.

There is one other variant of the outer join, one that tends to be rarely used. The full outer join retrieves all rows from both tables and relates those that can be related. Unlike a left outer join or right outer join, which includes unrelated rows from a single table, the full outer join includes unrelated rows from both tables. The syntax for a full outer join is as follows:

Input ▼

```
SELECT Customers.cust_id, Orders.order_num
FROM Customers
 FULL OUTER JOIN Orders ON Customers.cust_id = Orders.cust_id;
```

> CAUTION: **FULL OUTER JOIN Support**
> The FULL OUTER JOIN syntax is not supported by MariaDB, MySQL, or SQLite.

Using Joins with Aggregate Functions

As you learned in Lesson 9, "Summarizing Data," aggregate functions are used to summarize data. Although all the examples of aggregate functions thus far only summarized data from a single table, these functions can also be used with joins.

To demonstrate this, let's look at an example. You want to retrieve a list of all customers and the number of orders that each has placed. The following code uses the COUNT() function to achieve this:

Input ▼

```
SELECT Customers.cust_id,
       COUNT(Orders.order_num) AS num_ord
FROM Customers
 INNER JOIN Orders ON Customers.cust_id = Orders.cust_id
GROUP BY Customers.cust_id;
```

Output ▼

```
cust_id       num_ord
----------    --------
1000000001    2
1000000003    1
1000000004    1
1000000005    1
```

Analysis ▼

This SELECT statement uses INNER JOIN to relate the Customers and Orders tables to each other. The GROUP BY clause groups the data by customer, and so the function call COUNT(Orders.order_num) counts the number of orders for each customer and returns it as num_ord.

Aggregate functions can be used just as easily with other join types. See the following example:

Input ▼

```
SELECT Customers.cust_id,
       COUNT(Orders.order_num) AS num_ord
FROM Customers
 LEFT OUTER JOIN Orders ON Customers.cust_id = Orders.cust_id
 GROUP BY Customers.cust_id;
```

Output ▼

```
cust_id        num_ord
----------     -------
1000000001     2
1000000002     0
1000000003     1
1000000004     1
1000000005     1
```

Analysis ▼

This example uses a left outer join to include all customers, even those who have not placed any orders. The results show that customer 1000000002 with 0 orders is included this time, unlike when the INNER JOIN was used.

Using Joins and Join Conditions

Before I wrap up our two-lesson discussion on joins, I think it is worthwhile to summarize some key points regarding joins and their use:

▶ Pay careful attention to the type of join being used. More often than not, you'll want an inner join, but there are often valid uses for outer joins too.

- ▶ Check your DBMS documentation for the exact join syntax it supports. (Most DBMSs use one of the forms of syntax described in these two lessons.)

- ▶ Make sure you use the correct join condition (regardless of the syntax being used), or you'll return incorrect data.

- ▶ Make sure you always provide a join condition, or you'll end up with the Cartesian product.

- ▶ You may include multiple tables in a join and even have different join types for each. Although this is legal and often useful, make sure you test each join separately before testing them together. This will make troubleshooting far simpler.

Summary

This lesson was a continuation of the last lesson on joins. This lesson started by teaching you how and why to use aliases, and then continued with a discussion on different join types and various forms of syntax used with each. You also learned how to use aggregate functions with joins and some important do's and dont's to keep in mind when working with joins.

Challenges

1. Write a SQL statement using an INNER JOIN to retrieve customer name (cust_name in Customers) and all order numbers (order_num in Orders) for each.

2. Modify the SQL statement you just created to list all customers, even those with no orders.

3. Use an OUTER JOIN to join the Products and OrderItems tables, returning a sorted list of product names (prod_name) and the order numbers (order_num) associated with each.

4. Modify the SQL statement created in the previous challenge so that it returns a total of number of orders for each item (as opposed to the order numbers).

5. Write a SQL statement to list vendors (vend_id in Vendors) and the number of products they have available, including vendors with no products. You'll want to use an OUTER JOIN and the COUNT() aggregate function to count the number of products for each in the Products table. Pay attention: the vend_id column appears in multiple tables, so any time you refer to it, you'll need to fully qualify it.

LESSON 14

Combining Queries

In this lesson, you'll learn how to use the UNION *operator to combine multiple* SELECT *statements into one result set.*

Understanding Combined Queries

Most SQL queries contain a single SELECT statement that returns data from one or more tables. SQL also enables you to perform multiple queries (multiple SELECT statements) and return the results as a single query result set. These combined queries are usually known as *unions* or *compound queries*.

There are basically two scenarios in which you'd use combined queries:

▶ To return similarly structured data from different tables in a single query

▶ To perform multiple queries against a single table returning the data as one query

---

TIP: **Combining Queries and Multiple** WHERE **Conditions**
For the most part, combining two queries to the same table accomplishes the same thing as a single query with multiple WHERE clause conditions. In other words, any SELECT statement with multiple WHERE clauses can also be specified as a combined query, as you'll see in the section that follows.

Creating Combined Queries

SQL queries are combined using the UNION operator. Using UNION, you can specify multiple SELECT statements, and their results can be combined into a single result set.

Using UNION

Using UNION is simple enough. All you do is specify each SELECT statement and place the keyword UNION between each.

Let's look at an example. You need a report on all your customers in Illinois, Indiana, and Michigan. You also want to include all Fun4All locations, regardless of state. Of course, you can create a WHERE clause that will do this, but this time you'll use a UNION instead.

As just explained, creating a UNION involves writing multiple SELECT statements. First, look at the individual statements:

Input ▼

```
SELECT cust_name, cust_contact, cust_email
FROM Customers
WHERE cust_state IN ('IL','IN','MI');
```

Output ▼

```
cust_name        cust_contact     cust_email
-----------      -------------    -----------
Village Toys     John Smith       sales@villagetoys.com
Fun4All          Jim Jones        jjones@fun4all.com
The Toy Store    Kim Howard       NULL
```

Input ▼

```
SELECT cust_name, cust_contact, cust_email
FROM Customers
WHERE cust_name = 'Fun4All';
```

Output ▼

```
cust_name       cust_contact        cust_email
-----------     -----------         -------------
Fun4All         Jim Jones           jjones@fun4all.com
Fun4All         Denise L. Stephens  dstephens@fun4all.com
```

Analysis ▼

The first SELECT retrieves all rows in Illinois, Indiana, and Michigan by passing those state abbreviations to the IN clause. The second SELECT uses a simple equality test to find all Fun4All locations. You'll notice that one row appears on both outputs as it meets both WHERE conditions.

To combine these two statements, do the following:

Input ▼

```
SELECT cust_name, cust_contact, cust_email
FROM Customers
WHERE cust_state IN ('IL','IN','MI')
UNION
SELECT cust_name, cust_contact, cust_email
FROM Customers
WHERE cust_name = 'Fun4All';
```

Output ▼

cust_name	cust_contact	cust_email
Fun4All	Denise L. Stephens	dstephens@fun4all.com
Fun4All	Jim Jones	jjones@fun4all.com
Village Toys	John Smith	sales@villagetoys.com
The Toy Store	Kim Howard	NULL

Analysis ▼

The preceding statements are made up of both of the previous SELECT statements separated by the UNION keyword. UNION instructs the DBMS to execute both SELECT statements and combine the output into a single query result set.

As a point of reference, here is the same query using multiple WHERE clauses instead of a UNION:

Input ▼

```
SELECT cust_name, cust_contact, cust_email
FROM Customers
WHERE cust_state IN ('IL','IN','MI')
UNION
SELECT cust_name, cust_contact, cust_email
FROM Customers
WHERE cust_name = 'Fun4All';
```

In our simple example, the UNION might actually be more complicated than using a WHERE clause. But with more complex filtering conditions, or if the data is being retrieved from multiple tables (and not just a single table), the UNION could have made the process much simpler indeed.

TIP: UNION **Limits**

There is no standard SQL limit to the number of SELECT statements that can be combined with UNION statements. However, it is best to consult your DBMS documentation to ensure that it does not enforce any maximum statement restrictions of its own.

CAUTION: **Performance Issues**

Most good DBMSs use an internal query optimizer to combine the SELECT statements before they are even processed. In theory, this means that from a performance perspective, there should be no real difference between using multiple WHERE clause conditions or a UNION. I say in theory, because, in practice, most query optimizers don't always do as good a job as they should. Your best bet is to test both methods to see which will work best for you.

UNION **Rules**

As you can see, unions are very easy to use. But there are a few rules governing exactly which can be combined:

▶ A UNION must be composed of two or more SELECT statements, each separated by the keyword UNION (so, if you're combining four SELECT statements, you would use three UNION keywords).

▶ Each query in a UNION must contain the same columns, expressions, or aggregate functions (and some DBMSs even require that columns be listed in the same order).

▶ Column datatypes must be compatible. They need not be the same name or the exact same type, but they must be of a type that the DBMS can implicitly convert (for example, different numeric types or different date types).

If SELECT statements that are combined with a UNION have different column names, what name is actually returned? For example, if one statement contained SELECT prod_name and the next used SELECT productname, what would be the name of the combined returned column?

The answer is that the first name is used, so in our example the combined column would be named prod_name, even though the second SELECT used a different name. This also means that you can use an alias on the first name to set the returned column name as needed.

This behavior has another interesting side effect. Because the first set of column names are used, only those names can be specified when sorting. Again, in our example, you could use ORDER BY prod_name to sort the combined results, but ORDER BY productname would display an error message because there is no column productname in the combined results.

Aside from these basic rules and restrictions, unions can be used for any data retrieval tasks.

Including or Eliminating Duplicate Rows

Go back to the preceding section titled "Using UNION" and look at the sample SELECT statements used. You'll notice that when executed individually, the first SELECT statement returns three rows, and the second SELECT statement returns two rows. However, when the two SELECT statements are combined with a UNION, only four rows are returned, not five.

The UNION automatically removes any duplicate rows from the query result set (in other words, it behaves just as multiple WHERE clause conditions in a single SELECT would). Because there is a Fun4All location in Indiana, that row was returned by both SELECT statements. When the UNION was used, the duplicate row was eliminated.

This is the default behavior of UNION, but you can change it if you so desire. If you would, in fact, want all occurrences of all matches returned, you could use UNION ALL instead of UNION.

Look at the following example:

Input ▼

```
SELECT cust_name, cust_contact, cust_email
FROM Customers
WHERE cust_state IN ('IL','IN','MI')
UNION ALL
SELECT cust_name, cust_contact, cust_email
FROM Customers
WHERE cust_name = 'Fun4All';
```

Output ▼

```
cust_name        cust_contact          cust_email
-----------      -------------         ------------
Village Toys     John Smith            sales@villagetoys.com
Fun4All          Jim Jones             jjones@fun4all.com
The Toy Store    Kim Howard            NULL
Fun4All          Jim Jones             jjones@fun4all.com
Fun4All          Denise L. Stephens    dstephens@fun4all.com
```

Analysis ▼

When you use UNION ALL, the DBMS does not eliminate duplicates. Therefore, the preceding example returns five rows, one of them occurring twice.

> TIP: UNION **Versus** WHERE
>
> At the beginning of this lesson, I said that UNION almost always accomplishes the same thing as multiple WHERE conditions. UNION ALL is the form of UNION that accomplishes what cannot be done with WHERE clauses. If you do, in fact, want all occurrences of matches for every condition (including duplicates), you must use UNION ALL and not WHERE.

Sorting Combined Query Results

SELECT statement output is sorted using the ORDER BY clause. When combining queries with a UNION, you may use only one ORDER BY clause, and it must occur after the final SELECT statement. There is very little point in sorting part of a result set one way and part another way, and so multiple ORDER BY clauses are not allowed.

The following example sorts the results returned by the previously used UNION:

Input ▼

```
SELECT cust_name, cust_contact, cust_email
FROM Customers
WHERE cust_state IN ('IL','IN','MI')
UNION
SELECT cust_name, cust_contact, cust_email
FROM Customers
WHERE cust_name = 'Fun4All'
ORDER BY cust_name, cust_contact;
```

Output ▼

```
cust_name        cust_contact        cust_email
----------       -------------       -------------
Fun4All          Denise L. Stephens  dstephens@fun4all.com
Fun4All          Jim Jones           jjones@fun4all.com
The Toy Store    Kim Howard          NULL
Village Toys     John Smith          sales@villagetoys.com
```

Analysis ▼

This UNION takes a single ORDER BY clause after the final SELECT statement. Even though the ORDER BY appears to be a part of only that last SELECT statement, the DBMS will in fact use it to sort all the results returned by all the SELECT statements.

> NOTE: **Other UNION Types**
>
> Some DBMSs support two additional types of UNION. EXCEPT (sometimes called MINUS) can be used to retrieve only the rows that exist in the first table but not in the second, and INTERSECT can be used to retrieve only the rows that exist in both tables. In practice, however, these UNION types are rarely used because the same results can be accomplished using joins.

> TIP: **Working with Multiple Tables**
>
> For simplicity's sake, the examples in this lesson have all used UNION to combine multiple queries on the same table. In practice, UNION is really useful when you need to combine data from multiple tables, even tables with mismatched column names, in which case you can combine UNION with aliases to retrieve a single set of results.

Summary

In this lesson, you learned how to combine SELECT statements with the UNION operator. Using UNION, you can return the results of multiple queries as one combined query, either including or excluding duplicates. The use of UNION can greatly simplify complex WHERE clauses and retrieval of data from multiple tables.

Challenges

1. Write a SQL statement that combines two SELECT statements that retrieve product ID (prod_id) and quantity from the OrderItems table, one filtering for rows with a quantity of exactly 100, and the other filtering for products with an ID that begins with BNBG. Sort the results by product ID.

2. Rewrite the SQL statement you just created to use a single SELECT statement.

3. This one is a little nonsensical, I know, but it does reinforce a note earlier in this lesson. Write a SQL statement which returns and combines product name (prod_name) from Products and customer name (cust_name) from Customers, and sort the result by product name.

4. What is wrong with the following SQL statement? (Try to figure it out without running it.)

```
SELECT cust_name, cust_contact, cust_email
FROM Customers
WHERE cust_state  = 'MI'
ORDER BY cust_name;
UNION
SELECT cust_name, cust_contact, cust_email
FROM Customers
WHERE cust_state = 'IL'ORDER BY cust_name;
```

LESSON 15

Inserting Data

In this lesson, you will learn how to insert data into tables using the SQL INSERT *statement.*

Understanding Data Insertion

SELECT is undoubtedly the most frequently used SQL statement (which is why the last 14 lessons were dedicated to it). But there are three other frequently used SQL statements that you should learn. The first one is INSERT. (You'll get to the other two in the next lesson.)

As its name suggests, INSERT is used to insert (add) rows to a database table. Insert can be used in several ways:

- ▶ Inserting a single complete row
- ▶ Inserting a single partial row
- ▶ Inserting the results of a query

Let's now look at each of these.

> TIP: INSERT **and System Security**
> Use of the INSERT statement might require special security privileges in client/server DBMSs. Before you attempt to use INSERT, make sure you have adequate security privileges to do so.

Inserting Complete Rows

The simplest way to insert data into a table is to use the basic INSERT syntax, which requires that you specify the table name and the values to be inserted into the new row. Here is an example of this:

Input ▼

```
INSERT INTO Customers
VALUES(1000000006,
       'Toy Land',
       '123 Any Street',
       'New York',
       'NY',
       '11111',
       'USA',
       NULL,
       NULL);
```

Analysis ▼

The above example inserts a new customer into the Customers table. The data to be stored in each table column is specified in the VALUES clause, and a value must be provided for every column. If a column has no value (for example, the cust_contact and cust_email columns above), the NULL value should be used (assuming the table allows no value to be specified for that column). The columns must be populated in the order in which they appear in the table definition.

> TIP: **The INTO Keyword**
> In some SQL implementations, the INTO keyword following INSERT is optional. However, it is good practice to provide this keyword even if it is not needed. Doing so will ensure that your SQL code is portable between DBMSs.

Although this syntax is indeed simple, it is not at all safe and should generally be avoided at all costs. The above SQL statement is highly dependent on the order in which the columns are defined in the table. It also depends on information about that order being readily available. Even if it is available, there is no guarantee that the columns will be in the exact same order the next time the table is reconstructed. Therefore, writing SQL statements that depend on specific column ordering is very unsafe. If you do so, something will inevitably break at some point.

The safer (and unfortunately more cumbersome) way to write the INSERT statement is as follows:

Input ▼

```
INSERT INTO Customers(cust_id,
                      cust_name,
                      cust_address,
                      cust_city,
                      cust_state,
                      cust_zip,
                      cust_country,
                      cust_contact,
                      cust_email)
VALUES(1000000006,
       'Toy Land',
       '123 Any Street',
       'New York',
       'NY',
       '11111',
       'USA',
       NULL,
       NULL);
```

Analysis ▼

This example does the exact same thing as the previous INSERT statement, but this time the column names are explicitly stated in parentheses after the table name. When the row is inserted, the DBMS will match each item in the columns list with the appropriate value in the VALUES list. The first entry in VALUES corresponds to the first specified column name. The second value corresponds to the second column name, and so on.

Because column names are provided, the VALUES must match the specified column names in the order in which they are specified, and not necessarily in the order that the columns appear in the actual table. The advantage of this is that, even if the table layout changes, the INSERT statement will still work correctly.

> NOTE: **Can't INSERT Same Record Twice**
>
> If you tried both versions of this example, you'll have discovered that the second generated an error because a customer with an ID of 1000000006 already existed. As discussed in Lesson 1, "Understanding SQL," primary key values must be unique, and because cust_id is the primary key, the DBMS won't allow you to insert two rows with the same cust_id value. The same is true for the next example. To try the other INSERT statements, you'd need to delete the first row added (as will be shown in the next Lesson). Or don't, because the row has been inserted and you can continue the lessons without deleting it.

The following INSERT statement populates all the row columns (just as before), but it does so in a different order. Because the column names are specified, the insertion will work correctly:

Input ▼

```
INSERT INTO Customers(cust_id,
                      cust_contact,
                      cust_email,
                      cust_name,
                      cust_address,
                      cust_city,
                      cust_state,
                      cust_zip)
VALUES(1000000006,
       NULL,
       NULL,
       'Toy Land',
       '123 Any Street',
       'New York',
       'NY',
       '11111');
```

> TIP: **Always Use a Columns List**
>
> As a rule, never use INSERT without explicitly specifying the column list. This will greatly increase the probability that your SQL will continue to function in the event that table changes occur.

> CAUTION: **Use VALUES Carefully**
>
> Regardless of the INSERT syntax being used, the correct number of VALUES must be specified. If no column names are provided, a value must be present for every table column. If column names are provided, a value must be present for each listed column. If none is present, an error message will be generated, and the row will not be inserted.

Inserting Partial Rows

As I just explained, the recommended way to use INSERT is to explicitly specify table column names. Using this syntax, you can also omit columns. This means you provide values for only some columns, but not for others.

Look at the following example:

Input ▼

```
INSERT INTO Customers(cust_id,
                      cust_name,
                      cust_address,
                      cust_city,
                      cust_state,
                      cust_zip,
                      cust_country)
VALUES(1000000006,
       'Toy Land',
       '123 Any Street',
       'New York',
       'NY',
       '11111',
       'USA');
```

Analysis ▼

In the examples given earlier in this lesson, values were not provided for two of the columns, cust_contact and cust_email. This means there is no reason to include those columns in the INSERT statement. This INSERT statement, therefore, omits the two columns and the two corresponding values.

CAUTION: **Omitting Columns**

You may omit columns from an INSERT operation if the table definition so allows. One of the following conditions must exist:

▶ The column is defined as allowing NULL values (no value at all).

▶ A default value is specified in the table definition. This means the default value will be used if no value is specified.

CAUTION: **Omitting Required Values**

If you omit a value from a table that does not allow NULL values and does not have a default, the DBMS will generate an error message, and the row will not be inserted.

Inserting Retrieved Data

INSERT is usually used to add a row to a table using specified values. There is another form of INSERT that can be used to insert the result of a SELECT statement into a table. This is known as INSERT SELECT, and, as its name suggests, it is made up of an INSERT statement and a SELECT statement.

Suppose you want to merge a list of customers from another table into your Customers table. Instead of reading one row at a time and inserting it with INSERT, you can do the following:

Input ▼

```
INSERT INTO Customers(cust_id,
                      cust_contact,
                      cust_email,
                      cust_name,
                      cust_address,
                      cust_city,
                      cust_state,
                      cust_zip,
                      cust_country)
SELECT cust_id,
       cust_contact,
       cust_email,
       cust_name,
       cust_address,
       cust_city,
       cust_state,
       cust_zip,
       cust_country
FROM CustNew;
```

NOTE: **Instructions Needed for the Next Example**

The following example imports data from a table named CustNew into the Customers table. To try this example, create and populate the CustNew table first. The format of the CustNew table should be the same as the Customers table described in Appendix A, "Sample Table Scripts." When populating CustNew, be sure not to use cust_id values that were already used in Customers. (The subsequent INSERT operation fails if primary key values are duplicated.)

Analysis ▼

This example uses INSERT SELECT to import all the data from CustNew into Customers. Instead of listing the VALUES to be inserted, the SELECT statement retrieves them from CustNew. Each column in the SELECT corresponds to a column in the specified columns list. How many rows will this statement insert? That depends on how many rows are in the CustNew table. If the table is empty, no rows will be inserted (and no error will be generated because the operation is still valid). If the table does, in fact, contain data, all that data will be inserted into Customers.

> TIP: **Column Names in INSERT SELECT**
>
> This example uses the same column names in both the INSERT and SELECT statements for simplicity's sake. But there is no requirement that the column names match. In fact, the DBMS does not even pay attention to the column names returned by the SELECT. Rather, the column position is used, so the first column in the SELECT statement (regardless of its name) will be used to populate the first specified table column, and so on.

The SELECT statement used in an INSERT SELECT can include a WHERE clause to filter the data to be inserted.

> TIP: **Inserting Multiple Rows**
>
> INSERT usually inserts only a single row. To insert multiple rows, you must execute multiple INSERT statements. The exception to this rule is INSERT SELECT, which can be used to insert multiple rows with a single statement; whatever the SELECT statement returns will be inserted by the INSERT.

Copying from One Table to Another

There is another form of data insertion that does not use the INSERT statement at all. To copy the contents of a table into a brand new table (one that is created on the fly), you can use the CREATE SELECT statement (or SELECT INTO if using SQL Server).

> NOTE: **Not Supported by DB2**
>
> DB2 does not support the use of CREATE SELECT as described here.

Unlike INSERT SELECT, which appends data to an existing table, CREATE SELECT copies data into a new table (and, depending on the DBMS being used, can overwrite the table if it already exists).

The following example demonstrates the use of CREATE SELECT:

Input ▼

```
CREATE TABLE CustCopy AS SELECT * FROM Customers;
```

If using SQL Server, use this syntax instead:

Input ▼

```
SELECT * INTO CustCopy FROM Customers;
```

Analysis ▼

This SELECT statement creates a new table named CustCopy and copies the entire contents of the Customers table into it. Because SELECT * was used, every column in the Customers table will be created (and populated) in the CustCopy table. To copy only a subset of the available columns, you can specify explicit column names instead of the * wildcard character.

Here are some things to consider when using SELECT INTO:

▶ Any SELECT options and clauses may be used, including WHERE and GROUP BY.

▶ Joins may be used to insert data from multiple tables.

▶ Data may only be inserted into a single table regardless of how many tables the data was retrieved from.

TIP: **Making Copies of Tables**

The technique described here is a great way to make copies of tables before experimenting with new SQL statements. By making a copy first, you'll be able to test your SQL on that copy instead of on live data.

NOTE: **More Examples**

Looking for more examples of INSERT usage? See the example table population scripts described in Appendix A.

Summary

In this lesson, you learned how to insert rows into a database table using INSERT. You learned several ways to use INSERT and why explicit column specification is preferred. You also learned how to use INSERT SELECT to import rows from another table and how to use SELECT INTO to export rows to a new table. In the next lesson, you'll learn how to use UPDATE and DELETE to further manipulate table data.

Challenges

1. Using INSERT and columns specified, add yourself to the Customers table. Explicitly list the columns you are adding and only the ones you need.

2. Make backup copies of your Orders and OrderItems tables.

LESSON 16

Updating and Deleting Data

In this lesson, you will learn how to use the UPDATE *and* DELETE *statements to enable you to further manipulate your table data.*

Updating Data

To update (modify) data in a table, you use the UPDATE statement. UPDATE can be used in two ways:

▶ To update specific rows in a table

▶ To update all rows in a table

You'll now take a look at each of these uses.

> CAUTION: **Don't Omit the WHERE Clause**
>
> Special care must be exercised when using UPDATE because it is all too easy to mistakenly update every row in your table. Please read this entire section on UPDATE before using this statement.

> TIP: UPDATE **and Security**
>
> Use of the UPDATE statement might require special security privileges in client/server DBMSs. Before you attempt to use UPDATE, make sure you have adequate security privileges to do so.

The UPDATE statement is very easy to use—some would say too easy. The basic format of an UPDATE statement is made up of three parts:

▶ The table to be updated

▶ The column names and their new values

▶ The filter condition that determines which rows should be updated

Let's take a look at a simple example. Customer 1000000005 has no email address on file and now has an address, so that record needs updating. The following statement performs this update:

Input ▼

```
UPDATE Customers
SET cust_email = 'kim@thetoystore.com'
WHERE cust_id = 1000000005;
```

The UPDATE statement always begins with the name of the table being updated. In this example, it is the Customers table. The SET command is then used to assign the new value to a column. As used here, the SET clause sets the cust_email column to the specified value:

```
SET cust_email = 'kim@thetoystore.com'
```

The UPDATE statement finishes with a WHERE clause that tells the DBMS which row to update. Without a WHERE clause, the DBMS would update all the rows in the Customers table with this new email address—definitely not the desired outcome.

Updating multiple columns requires a slightly different syntax:

Input ▼

```
UPDATE Customers
SET cust_contact = 'Sam Roberts',
    cust_email = 'sam@toyland.com'
WHERE cust_id = 1000000006;
```

When you are updating multiple columns, you use only a single SET command, and each column = value pair is separated by a comma. (No comma is specified after the last column.) In this example, columns cust_contact and cust_email will both be updated for customer 1000000006.

> TIP: **Using Subqueries in an UPDATE Statement**
> Subqueries may be used in UPDATE statements, enabling you to update columns with data retrieved with a SELECT statement. Refer to Lesson 11, "Working with Subqueries," for more information on subqueries and their uses.

> TIP: **The FROM Keyword**
> Some SQL implementations support a FROM clause in the UPDATE statement that can be used to update the rows in one table with data from another table. Refer to your DBMS documentation to see if it supports this feature.

To delete a column's value, you can set it to NULL (assuming the table is defined to allow NULL values). You can do this as follows:

Input ▼

```
UPDATE Customers
SET cust_email = NULL
WHERE cust_id = 1000000005;
```

Here the NULL keyword is used to save no value to the cust_email column. That is very different from saving an empty string. An empty string (specified as ' ') is a value, whereas NULL means that there is no value at all.

Deleting Data

To delete (remove) data from a table, you use the DELETE statement. DELETE can be used in two ways:

▶ To delete specific rows from a table

▶ To delete all rows from a table

Now let's take a look at each of these.

CAUTION: **Don't Omit the WHERE Clause**

Special care must be exercised when using DELETE because it is all too easy to mistakenly delete every row from your table. Please read this entire section on DELETE before using this statement.

TIP: DELETE **and Security**

Use of the DELETE statement might require special security privileges in client/server DBMSs. Before you attempt to use DELETE, make sure you have adequate security privileges to do so.

I already stated that UPDATE is very easy to use. The good (and bad) news is that DELETE is even easier to use.

The following statement deletes a single row from the Customers table (the row you added in the last lesson):

Input ▼

```
DELETE FROM Customers
WHERE cust_id = 1000000006;
```

This statement should be self-explanatory. DELETE FROM requires that you specify the name of the table from which the data is to be deleted. The WHERE clause filters which rows are to be deleted. In this example, only customer 1000000006 will be deleted. If the WHERE clause were omitted, this statement would have deleted every customer in the table!

TIP: **Foreign Keys Are Your Friend**

Joins were introduced in Lesson 12, "Joining Tables," and as you learned then, to join two tables, you simply need common fields in both of those tables. But you can also have the DBMS enforce the relationship by using foreign keys. (These are defined in Appendix A, "Sample Table Scripts.") When foreign keys are present, the DBMS uses them to enforce referential integrity. For example, if you tried to insert a new product into the Products table, the DBMS would not allow you to insert it with an unknown vendor ID because the vend_id column is connected to the Vendors table as a foreign key. So what does this have to do with DELETE? Well, a nice side effect of using foreign keys to ensure referential integrity is that the DBMS usually prevents the deletion of rows that are needed for a relationship. For example, if you tried to delete a product from Products that was used in existing orders in OrderItems, that DELETE statement would throw an error and would be aborted. That's another reason to always define your foreign keys.

TIP: **The FROM Keyword**

In some SQL implementations, the FROM keyword following DELETE is optional. However, it is good practice to always provide this keyword, even if it is not needed. Doing this will ensure that your SQL code is portable between DBMSs.

DELETE takes no column names or wildcard characters. DELETE deletes entire rows, not columns. To delete specific columns, you use an UPDATE statement.

NOTE: **Table Contents, Not Tables**

The DELETE statement deletes rows from tables, even all rows from tables. But DELETE never deletes the table itself.

TIP: **Faster Deletes**

If you really do want to delete all rows from a table, don't use DELETE. Instead, use the TRUNCATE TABLE statement, which accomplishes the same thing but does it much quicker (because data changes are not logged).

Guidelines for Updating and Deleting Data

The UPDATE and DELETE statements used in the previous section all have WHERE clauses, and there is a very good reason for this. If you omit the WHERE clause, the UPDATE or DELETE will be applied to every row in the table. In other words, if you execute an UPDATE without a WHERE clause, every row in the table will be updated with the new values. Similarly, if you execute DELETE without a WHERE clause, all the contents of the table will be deleted.

Here are some important guidelines that many SQL programmers follow:

▶ Never execute an UPDATE or a DELETE without a WHERE clause unless you really do intend to update and delete every row.

▶ Make sure every table has a primary key (refer to Lesson 12 if you have forgotten what this is), and use it as the WHERE clause whenever possible. (You may specify individual primary keys, multiple values, or value ranges.)

▶ Before you use a WHERE clause with an UPDATE or a DELETE, first test it with a SELECT to make sure it is filtering the right records; it is far too easy to write incorrect WHERE clauses.

▶ Use database-enforced referential integrity (refer to Lesson 12 for this one too) so that the DBMS will not allow the deletion of rows that have data in other tables related to them.

▶ Some DBMSs allow database administrators to impose restrictions that prevent the execution of UPDATE or DELETE without a WHERE clause. If your DBMS supports this feature, consider using it.

The bottom line is that SQL has no Undo button. Be very careful using UPDATE and DELETE, or you'll find yourself updating and deleting the wrong data.

Summary

In this lesson, you learned how to use the UPDATE and DELETE statements to manipulate the data in your tables. You learned the syntax for each of these statements, as well as the inherent dangers they expose. You also learned why WHERE clauses are so important in UPDATE and DELETE statements, and you were given guidelines that should be followed to help ensure that data does not get damaged inadvertently.

Challenges

1. USA state abbreviations should always be in uppercase. Write a SQL statement to update all USA addresses, both vendor states (vend_state in Vendors) and customer states (cust_state in Customers), so that they are uppercase.

2. Lesson 15 Challenge 1 asked you to add yourself to the Customers table. Now delete yourself. Make sure to use a WHERE clause (and test it with a SELECT before using it in DELETE), or you'll delete all customers!

LESSON 17

Creating and Manipulating Tables

In this lesson, you'll learn the basics of table creation, alteration, and deletion.

Creating Tables

SQL is not used just for table data manipulation. Rather, SQL can be used to perform all database and table operations, including the creation and manipulation of tables themselves.

There are generally two ways to create database tables:

- ▶ Most DBMSs come with an administration tool that you can use to create and manage database tables interactively.

- ▶ Tables may also be manipulated directly with SQL statements.

To create tables programmatically, you use the CREATE TABLE SQL statement. It is worth noting that when you use interactive management tools, you are actually using SQL statements. Instead of your writing these statements, however, the interface generates and executes the SQL seamlessly for you (the same is true for changes to existing tables).

> CAUTION: **Syntax Differences**
>
> The exact syntax of the CREATE TABLE statement can vary from one SQL implementation to another. Be sure to refer to your DBMS documentation for more information on exactly what syntax and features it supports.

Complete coverage of all the options available when creating tables is beyond the scope of this lesson, but here are the basics. I recommend that you review your DBMS documentation for more information and specifics.

> NOTE: **DBMS-Specific Examples**
>
> For examples of DBMS-specific CREATE TABLE statements, see the example table creation scripts described in Appendix A, "Sample Table Scripts."

Basic Table Creation

To create a table using CREATE TABLE, you must specify the following information:

▶ The name of the new table specified after the keywords CREATE TABLE.

▶ The name and definition of the table columns separated by commas.

▶ Some DBMSs require that you also specify the table location (as in which specific database it is to be created).

The following SQL statement creates the Products table used throughout this book:

Input ▼

```
CREATE TABLE Products
(
    prod_id      CHAR(10)        NOT NULL,
    vend_id      CHAR(10)        NOT NULL,
    prod_name    CHAR(254)       NOT NULL,
    prod_price   DECIMAL(8,2)    NOT NULL,
    prod_desc    VARCHAR(1000)   NULL
);
```

Analysis ▼

As you can see in the above statement, the table name is specified immediately following the CREATE TABLE keywords. The actual table definition (all the columns) is enclosed within parentheses. The columns themselves are separated by commas. This particular table is made up of five columns. Each column definition starts with the column name (which must be unique within the table), followed by the column's datatype. (Refer to Lesson 1, "Understanding SQL," for an explanation of datatypes. In addition, Appendix C, "Using SQL Datatypes," lists commonly used datatypes and their compatibility.) The entire statement is terminated with a semicolon after the closing parenthesis.

I mentioned earlier that CREATE TABLE syntax varies greatly from one DBMS to another, and the simple script above demonstrates this. While the statement will work as is on most DBMSs, for DB2 the NULL must be removed from the final column. This is why I had to create a different SQL table creation script for each DBMS (as explained in Appendix A).

TIP: **Statement Formatting**

As you will recall, white space is ignored in SQL statements. Statements can be typed on one long line or broken up over many lines. It makes no difference at all. This enables you to format your SQL as best suits you. The preceding CREATE TABLE statement is a good example of SQL statement formatting: the code is specified over multiple lines, with the column definitions indented for easier reading and editing. Formatting your SQL in this way is entirely optional but highly recommended.

Working with NULL Values

Back in Lesson 4, "Filtering Data," you learned that NULL values are no values or the lack of a value. A column that allows NULL values also allows rows to be inserted with no value at all in that column. A column that does not allow NULL values does not accept rows with no value; in other words, that column will always be required when rows are inserted or updated.

Every table column is either a NULL column or a NOT NULL column, and that state is specified in the table definition at creation time. Take a look at the following example:

Input ▼

```
CREATE TABLE Orders
(
    order_num    INTEGER     NOT NULL,
    order_date   DATETIME    NOT NULL,
    cust_id      CHAR(10)    NOT NULL
);
```

Analysis ▼

This statement creates the Orders table used throughout this book. Orders contains three columns: the order number, order date, and customer ID. All three columns are required, and so each contains the keyword NOT NULL. This will prevent the insertion of columns with no value. If someone tries to insert no value, an error will be returned, and the insertion will fail.

This next example creates a table with a mixture of NULL and NOT NULL columns:

Input ▼

```
CREATE TABLE Vendors
(
    vend_id       CHAR(10)    NOT NULL,
    vend_name     CHAR(50)    NOT NULL,
    vend_address  CHAR(50)    ,
    vend_city     CHAR(50)    ,
    vend_state    CHAR(5)     ,
    vend_zip      CHAR(10)    ,
    vend_country  CHAR(50)
);
```

Analysis ▼

This statement creates the `Vendors` table used throughout this book. The vendor ID and vendor name columns are both required and are, therefore, specified as NOT NULL. The five remaining columns all allow NULL values, and so NOT NULL is not specified. NULL is the default setting, so if NOT NULL is not specified, NULL is assumed.

> CAUTION: **Specifying** NULL
>
> Most DBMSs treat the absence of NOT NULL to mean NULL. However, not all do. Some DBMSs require the keyword NULL and will generate an error if it is not specified. Refer to your DBMS documentation for complete syntax information.

> TIP: **Primary Keys and** NULL **Values**
>
> Back in Lesson 1, you learned that primary keys are columns whose values uniquely identify every row in a table. Only columns that do not allow NULL values can be used in primary keys. Columns that allow no value at all cannot be used as unique identifiers.

> CAUTION: **Understanding** NULL
>
> Don't confuse NULL values with empty strings. A NULL value is the lack of a value; it is not an empty string. If you were to specify ' ' (two single quotes with nothing in between them), that would be allowed in a NOT NULL column. An empty string is a valid value; it is not no value. NULL values are specified with the keyword NULL, not with an empty string.

Specifying Default Values

SQL enables you to specify default values to be used if no value is specified when a row is inserted. Default values are specified using the DEFAULT keyword in the column definitions in the CREATE TABLE statement.

Look at the following example:

Input ▼

```
CREATE TABLE OrderItems
(
    order_num      INTEGER        NOT NULL,
    order_item     INTEGER        NOT NULL,
    prod_id        CHAR(10)       NOT NULL,
    quantity       INTEGER        NOT NULL    DEFAULT 1,
    item_price     DECIMAL(8,2)   NOT NULL
);
```

Analysis ▼

This statement creates the `OrderItems` table that contains the individual items that make up an order. (The order itself is stored in the `Orders` table.) The `quantity` column contains the quantity for each item in an order. In this example, adding the text `DEFAULT 1` to the column description instructs the DBMS to use a quantity of `1` if no quantity is specified.

Default values are often used to store values in date or time stamp columns. For example, the system date can be used as a default date by specifying the function or variable used to refer to the system date. For example, MySQL users may specify `DEFAULT CURRENT_DATE()`, while Oracle users may specify `DEFAULT SYSDATE`, and SQL Server users may specify `DEFAULT GETDATE()`. Unfortunately, the command used to obtain the system date is different in just about every DBMS. Table 17.1 lists the syntax for some DBMSs. If yours is not listed here, consult your DBMS documentation.

TABLE 17.1 Obtaining the System Date

DBMS	Function/Variable
DB2	`CURRENT_DATE`
MySQL	`CURRENT_DATE() or Now()`
Oracle	`SYSDATE`
PostgreSQL	`CURRENT_DATE`
SQL Server	`GETDATE()`
SQLite	`date('now')`

> TIP: **Using `DEFAULT` Instead of `NULL` Values**
> Many database developers use `DEFAULT` values instead of `NULL` columns, especially in columns that will be used in calculations or data groupings.

Updating Tables

To update table definitions, you use the `ALTER TABLE` statement. Although all DBMSs support `ALTER TABLE`, what they allow you to alter varies dramatically from one to another. Here are some points to consider when using `ALTER TABLE`:

▶ Ideally, tables should never be altered after they contain data. You should spend sufficient time anticipating future needs during the table design process so that extensive changes are not required later on.

▶ All DBMSs allow you to add columns to existing tables, although some restrict the datatypes that may be added (as well as NULL and DEFAULT usage).

▶ Many DBMSs do not allow you to remove or change columns in a table.

▶ Most DBMSs allow you to rename columns.

▶ Many DBMSs restrict the kinds of changes you can make on columns that are populated and enforce fewer restrictions on unpopulated columns.

As you can see, making changes to existing tables is neither simple nor consistent. Be sure to refer to your own DBMS documentation to determine exactly what you can alter.

To change a table using ALTER TABLE, you must specify the following information:

▶ The name of the table to be altered after the keywords ALTER TABLE. (The table must exist; otherwise, an error will be generated.)

▶ The list of changes to be made.

Because adding columns to an existing table is about the only operation supported by all DBMSs, I'll use that for an example:

Input ▼

```
ALTER TABLE Vendors
ADD vend_phone CHAR(20);
```

Analysis ▼

This statement adds a column named vend_phone to the Vendors table. The datatype must be specified.

Other ALTER operations—for example, changing or dropping columns, or adding constraints or keys—use a similar syntax.

Note that the following example will not work with all DBMSs:

Input ▼

```
ALTER TABLE Vendors
DROP COLUMN vend_phone;
```

Complex table structure changes usually require a manual move process involving these steps:

1. Create a new table with the new column layout.

2. Use the INSERT SELECT statement (see Lesson 15, "Inserting Data," for details of this statement) to copy the data from the old table to the new table. Use conversion functions and calculated fields, if needed.

3. Verify that the new table contains the desired data.

4. Rename the old table (or delete it, if you are really brave).

5. Rename the new table with the name previously used by the old table.

6. Re-create any triggers, stored procedures, indexes, and foreign keys as needed.

NOTE: ALTER TABLE and SQLite

SQLite limits the operations that may be performed using ALTER TABLE. One of the most important limitations is that it does not support the use of ALTER TABLE to define primary and foreign keys; these must be specified at initial CREATE TABLE time.

CAUTION: Use ALTER TABLE Carefully

Use ALTER TABLE with extreme caution, and be sure you have a complete set of backups (both schema and data) before proceeding. Database table changes cannot be undone, and if you add columns you don't need, you might not be able to remove them. Similarly, if you drop a column that you do need, you might lose all the data in that column.

Deleting Tables

Deleting tables (actually removing the entire table, not just the contents) is very easy—arguably too easy. Tables are deleted using the DROP TABLE statement:

Input ▼

```
DROP TABLE CustCopy;
```

Analysis ▼

This statement deletes the `CustCopy` table. (You created that one in Lesson 15.) There is no confirmation, nor is there an undo. Executing the statement will permanently remove the table.

> TIP: **Using Relational Rules to Prevent Accidental Deletion**
>
> Many DBMSs allow you to enforce rules that prevent the dropping of tables that are related to other tables. When these rules are enforced, if you issue a `DROP TABLE` statement against a table that is part of a relationship, the DBMS blocks the operation until the relationship is removed. It is a good idea to enable these options, if available, to prevent the accidental dropping of needed tables.

Renaming Tables

Table renaming is supported differently by each DBMS. There is no hard-and-fast standard for this operation. DB2, MariaDB, MySQL, Oracle, and PostgreSQL users can use the `RENAME` statement. SQL Server users can use the supplied `sp_rename` stored procedure. SQLite supports the renaming of tables via the `ALTER TABLE` statement.

The basic syntax for all rename operations requires that you specify the old name and a new name; however, there are DBMS implementation differences. Refer to your own DBMS documentation for details on supported syntax.

Summary

In this lesson, you learned several new SQL statements. `CREATE TABLE` is used to create new tables, `ALTER TABLE` is used to change table columns (or other objects like constraints or indexes), and `DROP TABLE` is used to completely delete a table. These statements should be used with extreme caution and only after backups have been made. Because the exact syntax of each of these statements varies from one DBMS to another, you should consult your own DBMS documentation for more information.

Challenges

1. Add a website column (`vend_web`) to the `Vendors` table. You need a text field big enough to accommodate a URL.

2. Use UPDATE statements to update `Vendor` records to include a website (you can make up any address).

LESSON 18

Using Views

In this lesson, you'll learn exactly what views are, how they work, and when they should be used. You'll also see how views can be used to simplify some of the SQL operations performed in earlier lessons.

Understanding Views

Views are virtual tables. Unlike tables that contain data, views simply contain queries that dynamically retrieve data when used.

> NOTE: **Views in SQLite**
> SQLite supports only read-only views, so views may be created and read, but their contents cannot be updated.

The best way to understand views is to look at an example. Back in Lesson 12, "Joining Tables," you used the following SELECT statement to retrieve data from three tables:

Input ▼

```
SELECT cust_name, cust_contact
FROM Customers, Orders, OrderItems
WHERE Customers.cust_id = Orders.cust_id
 AND OrderItems.order_num = Orders.order_num
 AND prod_id = 'RGAN01';
```

That query was used to retrieve the customers who had ordered a specific product. Anyone needing this data would have to understand the table structure, as well as how to create the query and join the tables. To retrieve the same data for another product (or for multiple products), you would have to modify the last WHERE clause.

Now imagine that you could wrap that entire query in a virtual table called
`ProductCustomers`. You could then simply do the following to retrieve the
same data:

Input ▼

```
SELECT cust_name, cust_contact
FROM ProductCustomers
WHERE prod_id = 'RGAN01';
```

This is where views come into play. `ProductCustomers` is a view, and as a view, it
does not contain any columns or data. Instead, it contains a query—the same query
used above to join the tables properly.

> TIP: **DBMS Consistency**
> You'll be relieved to know that view creation syntax is supported pretty consis-
> tently by all the major DBMSs.

Why Use Views

You've already seen one use for views. Here are some other common uses:

- ▶ To reuse SQL statements.
- ▶ To simplify complex SQL operations. After the query is written, it can be
  reused easily, without having to know the details of the underlying query
  itself.
- ▶ To expose parts of a table instead of complete tables.
- ▶ To secure data. Users can be given access to specific subsets of tables
  instead of to entire tables.
- ▶ To change data formatting and representation. Views can return data
  formatted and presented differently from their underlying tables.

For the most part, after views are created, they can be used in the same way as tables.
You can perform SELECT operations, filter and sort data, join views to other views or
tables, and possibly even add and update data. (There are some restrictions on this last
item. More on that in a moment.)

The important thing to remember is views are just that—views into data stored
elsewhere. Views contain no data themselves, so the data they return is retrieved from
other tables. When data is added or changed in those tables, the views will return that
changed data.

> CAUTION: **Performance Issues**
>
> Because views contain no data, any retrieval needed to execute a query must be processed every time the view is used. If you create complex views with multiple joins and filters, or if you nest views, you may find that performance is dramatically degraded. Be sure you test execution before deploying applications that use views extensively.

View Rules and Restrictions

Before you create views yourself, you should be aware of some restrictions. Unfortunately, the restrictions tend to be very DBMS specific, so check your own DBMS documentation before proceeding.

Here are some of the most common rules and restrictions governing view creation and usage:

▶ Like tables, views must be uniquely named. (They cannot be named with the name of any other table or view.)

▶ There is no limit to the number of views that can be created.

▶ To create views, you must have security access. This level of access is usually granted by the database administrator.

▶ Views can be nested; that is, a view may be built using a query that retrieves data from another view. The exact number of nested levels allowed varies from DBMS to DBMS. (Nesting views may seriously degrade query performance, so test this thoroughly before using it in production environments.)

▶ Many DBMSs prohibit the use of the ORDER BY clause in view queries.

▶ Some DBMSs require that every column returned be named; this will require the use of aliases if columns are calculated fields. (See Lesson 7, "Creating Calculated Fields," for more information on column aliases.)

▶ Views cannot be indexed, nor can they have triggers or default values associated with them.

▶ Some DBMSs, like SQLite, treat views as read-only queries, meaning you can retrieve data from views but not write data back to the underlying tables. Refer to your DBMS documentation for details.

▶ Some DBMSs allow you to create views that do not allow rows to be inserted or updated if that insertion or update will cause that row to no longer be part of the view. For example, if you have a view that retrieves only customers with email addresses, updating a customer to remove his email address would make that customer fall out of the view. This is the default behavior and is allowed, but depending on your DBMS, you might be able to prevent this from occurring.

TIP: Refer to Your DBMS Documentation

That's a long list of rules, and your own DBMS documentation will likely contain additional rules too. It is worth taking the time to understand what restrictions you must adhere to before creating views.

Creating Views

So now that you know what views are (and the rules and restrictions that govern them), let's look at view creation.

Views are created using the CREATE VIEW statement. Like CREATE TABLE, CREATE VIEW can only be used to create a view that does not exist.

NOTE: Renaming Views

To remove a view, you use the DROP statement. The syntax is simply DROP VIEW viewname;.

To overwrite (or update) a view, you must first DROP it and then re-create it.

Using Views to Simplify Complex Joins

One of the most common uses of views is to hide complex SQL, and this often involves joins. Look at the following statement:

Input ▼

```
CREATE VIEW ProductCustomers AS
SELECT cust_name, cust_contact, prod_id
FROM Customers, Orders, OrderItems
WHERE Customers.cust_id = Orders.cust_id
 AND OrderItems.order_num = Orders.order_num;
```

Analysis ▼

This statement creates a view named ProductCustomers, which joins three tables to return a list of all customers who have ordered any product. If you were to use SELECT * FROM ProductCustomers, you'd list every customer who ordered anything.

To retrieve a list of customers who ordered product RGAN01, you can do the following:

Input ▼

```
SELECT cust_name, cust_contact
FROM ProductCustomers
WHERE prod_id = 'RGAN01';
```

Output ▼

```
cust_name              cust_contact
-----------------      -----------------
Fun4All                Denise L. Stephens
The Toy Store          Kim Howard
```

Analysis ▼

This statement retrieves specific data from the view by issuing a WHERE clause. When the DBMS processes the request, it adds the specified WHERE clause to any existing WHERE clauses in the view query so that the data is filtered correctly.

As you can see, views can greatly simplify the use of complex SQL statements. Using views, you can write the underlying SQL once and then reuse it as needed.

> TIP: **Creating Reusable Views**
>
> It is a good idea to create views that are not tied to specific data. For example, the view created above returns customers for all products, not just product RGAN01 (for which the view was first created). Expanding the scope of the view enables it to be reused, making it even more useful. It also eliminates the need for you to create and maintain multiple similar views.

Using Views to Reformat Retrieved Data

As mentioned above, another common use of views is for reformatting retrieved data. The following SQL Server SELECT statement (from Lesson 7) returns vendor name and location in a single combined calculated column:

Input ▼

```
SELECT RTRIM(vend_name) + ' (' + RTRIM(vend_country) + ')'
       AS vend_title
FROM Vendors
ORDER BY vend_name;
```

Output ▼

```
vend_title
-------------------------------------------------------------
Bear Emporium (USA)
Bears R Us (USA)
Doll House Inc. (USA)
Fun and Games (England)
Furball Inc. (USA)
Jouets et ours (France)
```

The following is the same statement, but using the || syntax (as explained back in Lesson 7):

Input ▼

```
SELECT RTRIM(vend_name) || ' (' || RTRIM(vend_country) || ')'
       AS vend_title
FROM Vendors
ORDER BY vend_name;
```

Output ▼

```
vend_title
-------------------------------------------------------------
Bear Emporium (USA)
Bears R Us (USA)
Doll House Inc. (USA)
Fun and Games (England)
Furball Inc. (USA)
Jouets et ours (France)
```

Now suppose that you regularly needed results in this format. Rather than perform the concatenation each time it was needed, you could create a view and use that instead. To turn this statement into a view, you can do the following:

Input ▼

```
CREATE VIEW VendorLocations AS
SELECT RTRIM(vend_name) + ' (' + RTRIM(vend_country) + ')'
       AS vend_title
FROM Vendors;
```

Here's the same statement using | | syntax:

Input ▼

```
CREATE VIEW VendorLocations AS
SELECT RTRIM(vend_name) || ' (' || RTRIM(vend_country) || ')'
       AS vend_title
FROM Vendors;
```

Analysis ▼

This statement creates a view using the exact same query as the previous SELECT statement. To retrieve the data to create all mailing labels, simply do the following:

Input ▼

```
SELECT * FROM VendorLocations;
```

Output ▼

```
vend_title
------------------------------------------------------------
Bear Emporium (USA)
Bears R Us (USA)
Doll House Inc. (USA)
Fun and Games (England)
Furball Inc. (USA)
Jouets et ours (France)
```

> **NOTE: SELECT Restrictions All Apply**
>
> Earlier in this lesson I stated that the syntax used to create views is rather consistent between DBMSs. So why multiple versions of statements? A view simply wraps a SELECT statement, and the syntax of that SELECT must adhere to all the rules and restrictions of the DBMS being used.

Using Views to Filter Unwanted Data

Views are also useful for applying common WHERE clauses. For example, you might want to define a CustomerEMailList view so that it filters out customers without email addresses. To do this, you can use the following statement:

Input ▼

```
CREATE VIEW CustomerEMailList AS
SELECT cust_id, cust_name, cust_email
FROM Customers
WHERE cust_email IS NOT NULL;
```

Analysis ▼

Obviously, when sending email to a mailing list, you'd want to ignore users who have no email address. The WHERE clause here filters out those rows that have NULL values in the cust_email columns so that they'll not be retrieved.

View CustomerEMailList can now be used like any table:

Input ▼

```
SELECT *
FROM CustomerEMailList;
```

Output ▼

```
cust_id       cust_name      cust_email
----------    ------------   ---------------------
1000000001    Village Toys   sales@villagetoys.com
1000000003    Fun4All        jjones@fun4all.com
1000000004    Fun4All        dstephens@fun4all.com
```

> **NOTE: WHERE Clauses and WHERE Clauses**
>
> If a WHERE clause is used when retrieving data from the view, the two sets of clauses (the one in the view and the one passed to it) will be combined automatically.

Using Views with Calculated Fields

Views are exceptionally useful for simplifying the use of calculated fields. The following SELECT statement was introduced in Lesson 7. It retrieves the order items for a specific order, calculating the expanded price for each item:

Input ▼

```
SELECT prod_id,
       quantity,
       item_price,
       quantity*item_price AS expanded_price
FROM OrderItems
WHERE order_num = 20008;
```

Output ▼

```
prod_id    quantity    item_price    expanded_price
--------   ---------   -----------   --------------
RGAN01     5           4.9900        24.9500
BR03       5           11.9900       59.9500
```

BNBG01	10	3.4900	34.9000
BNBG02	10	3.4900	34.9000
BNBG03	10	3.4900	34.9000

To turn this into a view, do the following:

Input ▼

```
CREATE VIEW OrderItemsExpanded AS
SELECT order_num,
       prod_id,
       quantity,
       item_price,
       quantity*item_price AS expanded_price
FROM OrderItems
```

To retrieve the details for order 20008 (the output above), do the following:

Input ▼

```
SELECT *
FROM OrderItemsExpanded
WHERE order_num = 20008;
```

Output ▼

order_num	prod_id	quantity	item_price	expanded_price
20008	RGAN01	5	4.99	24.95
20008	BR03	5	11.99	59.95
20008	BNBG01	10	3.49	34.90
20008	BNBG02	10	3.49	34.90
20008	BNBG03	10	3.49	34.90

As you can see, views are easy to create and even easier to use. Used correctly, views can greatly simplify complex data manipulation.

Summary

Views are virtual tables. They do not contain data, but instead, they contain queries that retrieve data as needed. Views provide a level of encapsulation around SQL SELECT statements and can be used to simplify data manipulation, as well as to reformat or secure underlying data.

Challenges

1. Create a view called CustomersWithOrders that contains all of the columns in Customers but includes only those who have placed orders. Hint: you can use JOIN on the Orders table to filter just the customers you want. Then use a SELECT to make sure you have the right data.

2. What is wrong with the following SQL statement? (Try to figure it out without running it.)

```
CREATE VIEW OrderItemsExpanded AS
SELECT order_num,
       prod_id,
       quantity,
       item_price,
       quantity*item_price AS expanded_price
FROM OrderItems
ORDER BY order_num;
```

Working with Stored Procedures

In this lesson, you'll learn what stored procedures are, why they are used, and how. You'll also look at the basic syntax for creating and using them.

Understanding Stored Procedures

Most of the SQL statements that we've used thus far are simple in that they use a single statement against one or more tables. Not all operations are that simple. Often, multiple statements will be needed to perform a complete operation. For example, consider the following scenario:

- ▶ To process an order, checks must be made to ensure that items are in stock.

- ▶ If items are in stock, they need to be reserved so that they are not sold to anyone else, and the available quantity must be reduced to reflect the correct amount in stock.

- ▶ Any items not in stock need to be ordered; this requires some interaction with the vendor.

- ▶ The customer needs to be notified as to which items are in stock (and can be shipped immediately) and which are backordered.

This is obviously not a complete example, and it is even beyond the scope of the example tables that we have been using in this book, but it will suffice to help make a point. Performing this process requires many SQL statements against many tables. In addition, the exact SQL statements that need to be performed and their order are not fixed; they can (and will) vary according to which items are in stock and which are not.

How would you write this code? You could write each of the SQL statements individually and execute other statements conditionally based on the result. You'd have to do this every time this processing was needed (and in every application that needed it).

You could create a stored procedure. Stored procedures are simply collections of one or more SQL statements saved for future use. You can think of them as batch files, although in truth they are more than that.

> NOTE: **Not in SQLite**
> SQLite does not support stored procedures.

> NOTE: **There's a Lot More to It**
> Stored procedures are complex, and full coverage of the subject requires more space than can be allocated here. Truthfully, there are entire books on the subject. This lesson will not teach you all you need to know about stored procedures. Rather, it is intended simply to introduce the subject so that you are familiar with what they are and what they can do. As such, the examples presented here provide syntax for Oracle and SQL Server only.

Understanding Why to Use Stored Procedures

Now that you know what stored procedures are, why use them? There are lots of reasons, but here are the primary ones:

- ▶ To simplify complex operations (as seen in the previous example) by encapsulating processes into a single easy-to-use unit.

- ▶ To ensure data consistency by not requiring that a series of steps be created over and over. If all developers and applications use the same stored procedure, then the same code will be used by all.

- ▶ To prevent errors; this is an extension of the preceding reason. The more steps that need to be performed, the more likely it is that errors will be introduced. Preventing errors ensures data consistency.

- ▶ To simplify change management. If tables, column names, or business logic (or just about anything) changes, then only the stored procedure code needs to be updated, and no one else will even need to be aware that changes were made.

- ▶ To ensure security; this is an extension of the preceding reason. Restricting access to underlying data via stored procedures reduces the chance of data corruption (unintentional or otherwise).

- ▶ To do less work to process the command. Because stored procedures are usually stored in a compiled form, the DBMS has to do less work. This results in improved performance.

▶ To write code that is more powerful and flexible. There are SQL language elements and features that are available only within single requests. Stored procedures can use them for this reason.

In other words, there are three primary benefits: simplicity, security, and performance. Obviously, all are extremely important. Before you run off to turn all your SQL code into stored procedures, here's the downside:

▶ Stored procedure syntax varies dramatically from one DBMS to the next. In fact, it is close to impossible to write truly portable stored procedures. Having said that, the stored procedure calls themselves (their names and how data is passed to them) can be kept relatively portable so that if you need to change to another DBMS, at least your client application code may not need changing.

▶ Stored procedures tend to be more complex to write than basic SQL statements, and writing them requires a greater degree of skill and experience. As a result, many database administrators restrict stored procedure creation rights as a security measure (primarily due to the previous bullet item).

Nonetheless, stored procedures are very useful and should be used. In fact, most DBMSs come with all sorts of stored procedures that are used for database and table management. Refer to your DBMS documentation for more information on these.

> **NOTE: Can't Write Them? You Can Still Use Them**
>
> Most DBMSs distinguish the security and access needed to write stored procedures from the security and access needed to execute them. This is a good thing; even if you can't (or don't want to) write your own stored procedures, you can still execute them when appropriate.

Executing Stored Procedures

Stored procedures are executed far more often than they are written, so we'll start there. The SQL statement to execute a stored procedure is simply EXECUTE. EXECUTE takes the name of the stored procedure and any parameters that need to be passed to it. Take a look at this example (you cannot actually run it because the stored procedure AddNewProduct does not exist):

Input ▼

```
EXECUTE AddNewProduct('JTS01',
                      'Stuffed Eiffel Tower',
                      6.49,
                      'Plush stuffed toy with
➥the text La Tour Eiffel in red white and blue');
```

Analysis ▼

Here a stored procedure named AddNewProduct is executed; it adds a new product to the Products table. AddNewProduct takes four parameters: the vendor ID (the primary key from the Vendors table), product name, price, and description. These four parameters match four expected variables within the stored procedure (defined as part of the stored procedure itself). The stored procedure adds a new row to the Products table and assigns these passed attributes to the appropriate columns.

In the Products table, you'll notice that another column needs a value—the prod_id column, which is the table's primary key. Why was this value not passed as an attribute to the stored procedure? To ensure that IDs are generated properly, it is safer to have that process automated (and not rely on end users). That is why a stored procedure is used in this example. This is what this stored procedure does:

- ▶ It validates the passed data, ensuring that all four parameters have values.

- ▶ It generates a unique ID to be used as the primary key.

- ▶ It inserts the new product into the Products table, storing the generated primary key and passed data in the appropriate columns.

This is the basic form of stored procedure execution. Depending on the DBMS used, other execution options include the following:

- ▶ Optional parameters, with default values assumed if a parameter is not provided

- ▶ Out-of-order parameters, specified in parameter=value pairs

- ▶ Output parameters, allowing the stored procedure to update a parameter for use in the executing application

- ▶ Data retrieved by a SELECT statement

- ▶ Return codes, enabling the stored procedure to return a value to the executing application

Creating Stored Procedures

As already explained, writing a stored procedure is not trivial. To give you a taste for what is involved, let's look at a simple example—a stored procedure that counts the number of customers in a mailing list who have email addresses.

Here is the Oracle version:

Input ▼

```
CREATE PROCEDURE MailingListCount (
  ListCount OUT INTEGER
)
IS
v_rows INTEGER;
BEGIN
    SELECT COUNT(*) INTO v_rows
    FROM Customers
    WHERE NOT cust_email IS NULL;
    ListCount := v_rows;
END;
```

Analysis ▼

This stored procedure takes a single parameter named ListCount. Instead of passing a value to the stored procedure, this parameter passes a value back from it. The keyword OUT is used to specify this behavior. Oracle supports parameters of types IN (those passed to stored procedures), OUT (those passed from stored procedures, as we've used here), and INOUT (those used to pass parameters to and from stored procedures). The stored procedure code itself is enclosed within BEGIN and END statements, and here a simple SELECT is performed to retrieve the customers with email addresses. Then ListCount (the output parameter passed) is set with the number of rows that were retrieved.

To invoke the Oracle example, you could do the following:

Input ▼

```
var ReturnValue NUMBER
EXEC MailingListCount(:ReturnValue);
SELECT ReturnValue;
```

Analysis ▼

This code declares a variable to hold whatever the stored procedure returns, executes the stored procedure, and then uses a SELECT to display the returned value.

Here's the Microsoft SQL Server version:

Input ▼

```
CREATE PROCEDURE MailingListCount
AS
DECLARE @cnt INTEGER
SELECT @cnt = COUNT(*)
FROM Customers
WHERE NOT cust_email IS NULL;
RETURN @cnt;
```

Analysis ▼

This stored procedure takes no parameters at all. The calling application retrieves the value by using SQL Server's return code support. Here a local variable named @cnt is declared using the DECLARE statement (all local variables in SQL Server are named starting with a @). This variable is then used in the SELECT statement so that it contains the value returned by the COUNT() function. Finally, the RETURN statement is used to return the count to the calling application as RETURN @cnt.

To invoke the SQL Server example, you could do the following:

Input ▼

```
DECLARE @ReturnValue INT
EXECUTE @ReturnValue=MailingListCount;
SELECT @ReturnValue;
```

Analysis ▼

This code declares a variable to hold whatever the stored procedure returns, executes the stored procedure, and then uses a SELECT to display the returned value.

Here's another example, this time to insert a new order in the Orders table. This is a SQL Server–only example, but it demonstrates some useful stored procedure uses and techniques:

Input ▼

```
CREATE PROCEDURE NewOrder @cust_id CHAR(10)
AS
-- Declare variable for order number
DECLARE @order_num INTEGER
-- Get current highest order number
SELECT @order_num=MAX(order_num)
FROM Orders
-- Determine next order number
```

```
SELECT @order_num=@order_num+1
-- Insert new order
INSERT INTO Orders(order_num, order_date, cust_id)
VALUES(@order_num, GETDATE(), @cust_id)
-- Return order number
RETURN @order_num;
```

Analysis ▼

This stored procedure creates a new order in the Orders table. It takes a single parameter—the ID of the customer placing the order. The other two table columns, the order number and order date, are generated automatically within the stored procedure itself. The code first declares a local variable to store the order number. Next, the current highest order number is retrieved (using a MAX() function) and incremented (using a SELECT statement). Then the order is inserted with an INSERT statement using the newly generated order number, the current system date (retrieved using the GETDATE() function), and the passed customer ID. Finally, the order number (which is needed to process order items) is returned as RETURN @order_num. Notice that the code is commented; this should always be done when writing stored procedures.

> **NOTE: Comment Your Code**
>
> All code should be commented, and stored procedures are no different. Adding comments will not affect performance at all, so there is no downside here (other than the time it takes to write them). The benefits are numerous and include making it easier for others (and yourself) to understand the code and safer to make changes at a later date.
>
> As noted in Lesson 2, "Retrieving Data," a common way to comment code is to precede it with -- (two hyphens). Some DBMSs support alternate comment syntax, but all support -- and so you are best off using that.

Here's a quite different version of the same SQL Server code:

Input ▼

```
CREATE PROCEDURE NewOrder @cust_id CHAR(10)
AS
-- Insert new order
INSERT INTO Orders(cust_id)
VALUES(@cust_id)
-- Return order number
SELECT order_num = @@IDENTITY;
```

Analysis ▼

This stored procedure also creates a new order in the Orders table. This time the DBMS itself generates the order number. Most DBMSs support this type of functionality; SQL Server refers to these auto-incrementing columns as Identity fields (other DBMSs use names such as Auto Number or Sequences). Again, a single parameter is passed—the customer ID of the customer placing the order. The order number and order date are not specified at all; the DBMS uses a default value for the date (the GETDATE() function), and the order number is generated automatically. How can you find out what the generated ID is? SQL Server makes that available in the global variable @@IDENTITY, which is returned to the calling application (this time using a SELECT statement).

As you can see, with stored procedures there are often many different ways to accomplish the same task. The method you choose will often be dictated by the features of the DBMS you are using.

Summary

In this lesson, you learned what stored procedures are and why they are used. You also learned the basics of stored procedure execution and creation syntax, and you saw some of the ways these can be used. Using stored procedures is a really important topic, and one that is far beyond the scope of one lesson. As you have seen here, stored procedures are implemented differently in each DBMS. In addition, your own DBMS probably offers some form of these functions, as well as others not mentioned here. Refer to your DBMS documentation for more details.

Managing Transaction Processing

In this lesson, you'll learn what transactions are and how to use COMMIT *and* ROLLBACK *statements to manage transaction processing.*

Understanding Transaction Processing

Transaction processing is used to maintain database integrity by ensuring that batches of SQL operations execute completely or not at all.

As explained back in Lesson 12, "Joining Tables," relational databases are designed so that data is stored in multiple tables to facilitate easier data manipulation, management, and reuse. Without going in to the hows and whys of relational database design, take it as a given that well-designed database schemas are relational to some degree.

The Orders tables that you've been using in the past 19 lessons are a good example of this. Orders are stored in two tables: Orders stores actual orders, and OrderItems stores the individual items ordered. These two tables are related to each other using unique IDs called primary keys (as discussed in Lesson 1, "Understanding SQL"). These tables, in turn, are related to other tables containing customer and product information.

The process of adding an order to the system is as follows:

1. Check if the customer is already in the database. If not, add him or her.

2. Retrieve the customer's ID.

3. Add a row to the Orders table associating it with the customer ID.

4. Retrieve the new order ID assigned in the Orders table.

5. Add one row to the OrderItems table for each item ordered, associating it with the Orders table by the retrieved ID (and with the Products table by product ID).

Now imagine that some database failure (for example, out of disk space, security restrictions, table locks) prevents this entire sequence from completing. What would happen to your data?

Well, if the failure occurred after the customer was added and before the `Orders` table was added, there is no real problem. It is perfectly valid to have customers without orders. When you run the sequence again, the inserted customer record will be retrieved and used. You can effectively pick up where you left off.

But what if the failure occurred after the `Orders` row was added but before the `OrderItems` rows were added? Now you'd have an empty order sitting in your database.

Worse, what if the system failed during adding the `OrderItems` rows? Now you'd end up with a partial order in your database, but you wouldn't know it.

How do you solve this problem? That's where transaction processing comes in. *Transaction processing* is a mechanism used to manage sets of SQL operations that must be executed in batches so as to ensure that databases never contain the results of partial operations. With transaction processing, you can ensure that sets of operations are not aborted mid-processing—they either execute in their entirety or not at all (unless explicitly instructed otherwise). If no error occurs, the entire set of statements is committed (written) to the database tables. If an error does occur, then a rollback (undo) can occur to restore the database to a known and safe state.

So, if we look at the same example, this is how the process would work:

1. Check if the customer is already in the database; if not, add him or her.

2. Commit the customer information.

3. Retrieve the customer's ID.

4. Add a row to the `Orders` table.

5. If a failure occurs while adding the row to `Orders`, roll back.

6. Retrieve the new order ID assigned in the `Orders` table.

7. Add one row to the `OrderItems` table for each item ordered.

8. If a failure occurs while adding rows to `OrderItems`, roll back all the `OrderItems` rows added and the `Orders` row.

When you're working with transactions and transaction processing, a few keywords will keep reappearing. Here are the terms you need to know:

- ▶ **Transaction**—A block of SQL statements

- ▶ **Rollback**—The process of undoing specified SQL statements

▶ **Commit**—Writing unsaved SQL statements to the database tables

▶ **Savepoint**—A temporary placeholder in a transaction set to which you can issue a rollback (as opposed to rolling back an entire transaction)

TIP: **Which Statements Can You Roll Back?**

Transaction processing is used to manage INSERT, UPDATE, and DELETE statements. You cannot roll back SELECT statements. (There would not be much point in doing so anyway.) You cannot roll back CREATE or DROP operations. These statements may be used in a transaction block, but if you perform a rollback, they will not be undone.

Controlling Transactions

Now that you know what transaction processing is, let's look at what is involved in managing transactions.

CAUTION: **Implementation Differences**

The exact syntax used to implement transaction processing differs from one DBMS to another. Refer to your DBMS documentation before proceeding.

The key to managing transactions involves breaking your SQL statements into logical chunks and explicitly stating when data should be rolled back and when it should not.

Some DBMSs require that you explicitly mark the start and end of transaction blocks. In SQL Server, for example, you can do the following (replacing ... with the actual code):

Input ▼

```
BEGIN TRANSACTION
...
COMMIT TRANSACTION
```

Analysis ▼

In this example, any SQL between the BEGIN TRANSACTION and COMMIT TRANSACTION statements must be executed entirely or not at all.

The equivalent code in MariaDB and MySQL is

Input ▼

```
START TRANSACTION
...
```

Oracle uses this syntax:

Input ▼

```
SET TRANSACTION
...
```

PostgreSQL uses the ANSI SQL syntax:

Input ▼

```
BEGIN
...
```

Other DBMSs use variations of the above. You'll notice that most implementations don't have an explicit end of transaction. Rather, the transaction exists until something terminates it, usually a COMMIT to save changes or a ROLLBACK to undo them, as will be explained next.

Using ROLLBACK

The SQL ROLLBACK command is used to roll back (undo) SQL statements, as seen in this next statement:

Input ▼

```
DELETE FROM Orders;
ROLLBACK;
```

Analysis ▼

In this example, a DELETE operation is performed and then undone using a ROLLBACK statement. Although not the most useful example, it does demonstrate that, within a transaction block, DELETE operations (like INSERT and UPDATE operations) are never final.

Using COMMIT

Usually, SQL statements are executed and written directly to the database tables. This is known as an *implicit commit*—the commit (write or save) operation happens automatically.

Within a transaction block, however, commits might not occur implicitly. This, too, is DBMS specific. Some DBMSs treat a transaction end as an implicit commit; others do not.

To force an explicit commit, you use the COMMIT statement. The following is a SQL Server example:

Input ▼

```
BEGIN TRANSACTION
DELETE OrderItems WHERE order_num = 12345
DELETE Orders WHERE order_num = 12345
COMMIT TRANSACTION
```

Analysis ▼

In this SQL Server example, order number 12345 is deleted entirely from the system. Because this involves updating two database tables, Orders and OrderItems, a transaction block is used to ensure that the order is not partially deleted. The final COMMIT statement writes the change only if no error occurred. If the first DELETE worked, but the second failed, the DELETE would not be committed.

To accomplish the same thing in Oracle, you can do the following:

Input ▼

```
SET TRANSACTION
DELETE OrderItems WHERE order_num = 12345;
DELETE Orders WHERE order_num = 12345;
COMMIT;
```

Using Savepoints

Simple ROLLBACK and COMMIT statements enable you to write or undo an entire transaction. Although this approach works for simple transactions, more complex transactions might require partial commits or rollbacks.

For example, the process of adding an order described previously is a single transaction. If an error occurs, you only want to roll back to the point before the Orders row was added. You do not want to roll back the addition to the Customers table (if there was one).

To support the rollback of partial transactions, you must be able to put placeholders at strategic locations in the transaction block. Then, if a rollback is required, you can roll back to one of the placeholders.

In SQL, these placeholders are called *savepoints*. To create one in MariaDB, MySQL, and Oracle, you use the SAVEPOINT statement, as follows:

Input ▼

```
SAVEPOINT delete1;
```

In SQL Server, you do the following:

Input ▼

```
SAVE TRANSACTION delete1;
```

Each savepoint takes a unique name that identifies it so that, when you roll back, the DBMS knows where you are rolling back to. To roll back to this savepoint, do the following in SQL Server:

Input ▼

```
ROLLBACK TRANSACTION delete1;
```

In MariaDB, MySQL, and Oracle, you can do the following:

Input ▼

```
ROLLBACK TO delete1;
```

The following is a complete SQL Server example:

Input ▼

```
BEGIN TRANSACTION
INSERT INTO Customers(cust_id, cust_name)
VALUES(1000000010, 'Toys Emporium');
SAVE TRANSACTION StartOrder;
INSERT INTO Orders(order_num, order_date, cust_id)
VALUES(20100,'2020/12/1',1000000010);
IF @@ERROR <> 0 ROLLBACK TRANSACTION StartOrder;
INSERT INTO OrderItems(order_num, order_item,
➥prod_id, quantity, item_price)
VALUES(20100, 1, 'BR01', 100, 5.49);
IF @@ERROR <> 0 ROLLBACK TRANSACTION StartOrder;
INSERT INTO OrderItems(order_num, order_item,
➥prod_id, quantity, item_price)
VALUES(20100, 2, 'BR03', 100, 10.99);
IF @@ERROR <> 0 ROLLBACK TRANSACTION StartOrder;
COMMIT TRANSACTION
```

Analysis ▼

Here four INSERT statements are enclosed within a transaction block. A savepoint is defined after the first INSERT so that, if any of the subsequent INSERT operations fail, the transaction is only rolled back that far. In SQL Server, a variable named @@ERROR can be inspected to see if an operation succeeded. (Other DBMSs use different functions or variables to return this information.) If @@ERROR returns a value other than 0, an error occurred, and the transaction will roll back to the savepoint. If the entire transaction is processed, a COMMIT will be issued to save the data.

> TIP: **The More Savepoints the Better**
> You can have as many savepoints as you'd like within your SQL code, and the more the better. Why? Because the more savepoints you have, the more flexibility you have in managing rollbacks exactly as you need them.

Summary

In this lesson, you learned that transactions are blocks of SQL statements that must be executed as a batch. You learned that COMMIT and ROLLBACK statements are used to explicitly manage when data is written and when it is undone. You also learned that savepoints provide a greater level of control over rollback operations. Transaction processing is a really important topic, and one that is far beyond the scope of one lesson. In addition, as you saw here, transaction processing is implemented differently in each DBMS. As such, you should refer to your DBMS documentation for further details.

LESSON 21

Using Cursors

In this lesson, you'll be introduced to cursors and how (and why) to use them.

Understanding Cursors

SQL retrieval operations work with sets of rows known as *result sets*. The rows returned are all the rows that match a SQL statement—zero or more of them. When you use simple SELECT statements, there is no way to get the first row, the next row, or the previous 10 rows. This is an integral part of how a relational DBMS works.

> NEW TERM: **Result Set**
> The results retrieved by a SQL query.

Sometimes you need to step through rows forward or backward and one or more at a time. This is what cursors are used for. A cursor is a database query stored on the DBMS server—not a SELECT statement, but the result set retrieved by that statement. Once the cursor is stored, applications can scroll or browse up and down through the data as needed.

> NOTE: **SQLite Support**
> SQLite supports a form of cursors called *steps*. The basic concepts described in this lesson apply to SQLite steps, but the syntax can be quite different.

Different DBMSs support different cursor options and features. Some of the more common ones are

▶ The capability to flag a cursor as read-only so that data can be read but not updated or deleted

▶ The capability to control the directional operations that can be performed (forward, backward, first, last, absolute position, relative position, and so on)

▶ The capability to flag some columns as editable and others as not editable

▶ Scope specification so as to be able to make the cursor accessible to the specific request that created it (a stored procedure, for example) or to all requests

▶ Instructing the DBMS to make a copy of the retrieved data (as opposed to pointing to the live data in the table) so that data does not change between the time the cursor is opened and the time it is accessed

Cursors are used primarily by interactive applications in which users need to scroll up and down through screens of data, browsing or making changes.

Working with Cursors

Using cursors involves several distinct steps:

▶ Before a cursor can be used, it must be declared (defined). This process does not actually retrieve any data, it merely defines the SELECT statement to be used and any cursor options.

▶ Once it is declared, the cursor must be opened for use. This process actually retrieves the data using the previously defined SELECT statement.

▶ With the cursor populated with data, individual rows can be fetched (retrieved) as needed.

▶ When it is done, the cursor must be closed and possibly deallocated (depending on the DBMS).

Once a cursor is declared, it may be opened and closed as often as needed. Once it is open, fetch operations can be performed as often as needed.

Creating Cursors

Cursors are created using the DECLARE statement, which differs from one DBMS to the next. DECLARE names the cursor and takes a SELECT statement, complete with WHERE and other clauses if needed. To demonstrate this, we'll create a cursor that retrieves all customers without email addresses, as part of an application enabling an operator to provide missing email addresses.

Here is the DB2, MariaDB, MySQL, and SQL Server version:

Input ▼

```
DECLARE CustCursor CURSOR
FOR
SELECT * FROM Customers
WHERE cust_email IS NULL;
```

Here is the Oracle and PostgreSQL version:

Input ▼

```
DECLARE CURSOR CustCursor
IS
SELECT * FROM Customers
WHERE cust_email IS NULL;
```

Analysis ▼

In both versions, the DECLARE statement is used to define and name the cursor—in this case, CustCursor. The SELECT statement defines a cursor containing all customers with no email address (a NULL value).

Now that the cursor is defined, it is ready to be opened.

Using Cursors

Cursors are opened using the OPEN CURSOR statement, which is so simple a statement that most DBMSs support exactly the same syntax:

Input ▼

```
OPEN CURSOR CustCursor
```

Analysis ▼

When the OPEN CURSOR statement is processed, the query is executed, and the retrieved data is stored for subsequent browsing and scrolling.

Now the cursor data can be accessed using the FETCH statement. FETCH specifies the rows to be retrieved, where they are to be retrieved from, and where they are to be stored (variable names, for example). The first example uses Oracle syntax to retrieve a single row from the cursor (the first row):

Input ▼

```
DECLARE TYPE CustCursor IS REF CURSOR
    RETURN Customers%ROWTYPE;
DECLARE CustRecord Customers%ROWTYPE
BEGIN
    OPEN CustCursor;
    FETCH CustCursor INTO CustRecord;
    CLOSE CustCursor;
END;
```

Analysis ▼

In this example, FETCH is used to retrieve the current row (it'll start at the first row automatically) into a declared variable named CustRecord. Nothing is done with the retrieved data.

In the next example (again, using Oracle syntax), the retrieved data is looped through from the first row to the last:

Input ▼

```
DECLARE TYPE CustCursor IS REF CURSOR
    RETURN Customers%ROWTYPE;
DECLARE CustRecord Customers%ROWTYPE
BEGIN
    OPEN CustCursor;
    LOOP
    FETCH CustCursor INTO CustRecord;
    EXIT WHEN CustCursor%NOTFOUND;
        . . .
    END LOOP;
    CLOSE CustCursor;
END;
```

Analysis ▼

Like the previous example, this example uses FETCH to retrieve the current row into a declared variable named CustRecord. Unlike the previous example, the FETCH here is within a LOOP so that it is repeated over and over. The code EXIT WHEN CustCursor%NOTFOUND causes processing to be terminated (exiting the loop) when there are no more rows to be fetched. This example also does no actual processing; in real-world code you'd replace the . . . placeholder with your own code.

Here's another example, this time using Microsoft SQL Server syntax:

Input ▼

```
DECLARE @cust_id CHAR(10),
        @cust_name CHAR(50),
        @cust_address CHAR(50),
        @cust_city CHAR(50),
        @cust_state CHAR(5),
        @cust_zip CHAR(10),
        @cust_country CHAR(50),
        @cust_contact CHAR(50),
        @cust_email CHAR(255)
```

```
OPEN CustCursor
FETCH NEXT FROM CustCursor
    INTO @cust_id, @cust_name, @cust_address,
         @cust_city, @cust_state, @cust_zip,
         @cust_country, @cust_contact, @cust_email
   . . .
WHILE @@FETCH_STATUS = 0
BEGIN

FETCH NEXT FROM CustCursor
        INTO @cust_id, @cust_name, @cust_address,
             @cust_city, @cust_state, @cust_zip,
             @cust_country, @cust_contact, @cust_email
. . .
END
CLOSE CustCursor
```

Analysis ▼

In this example, variables are declared for each of the retrieved columns, and the
FETCH statements retrieve a row and save the values into those variables. A WHILE loop
is used to loop through the rows, and the condition WHILE @@FETCH_STATUS = 0
causes processing to be terminated (exiting the loop) when there are no more rows to
be fetched. Again, this example does no actual processing; in real-world code you'd
replace the . . . placeholder with your own code.

Closing Cursors

As already mentioned and seen in the previous examples, cursors need to be closed
after they have been used. In addition, some DBMSs (such as SQL Server) require
that the resources used by the cursor be explicitly deallocated. Here's the DB2,
Oracle, and PostgreSQL syntax:

Input ▼

```
CLOSE CustCursor
```

Here's the Microsoft SQL Server version:

Input ▼

```
CLOSE CustCursor
DEALLOCATE CURSOR CustCursor
```

Analysis ▼

The CLOSE statement is used to close cursors; once a cursor is closed, it cannot be reused without being opened again. However, a cursor does not need to be declared again to be used; an OPEN statement is sufficient.

Summary

In this lesson, you were introduced to cursors, what they are, and why they are used. Your own DBMS probably offers some form of this function, as well as others not mentioned here. Refer to your DBMS documentation for more details.

LESSON 22

Understanding Advanced SQL Features

In this lesson, you'll look at several of the advanced data manipulation features that have evolved with SQL: constraints, indexes, and triggers.

Understanding Constraints

SQL has evolved through many versions to become a very complete and powerful language. Many of the more powerful features are sophisticated tools that provide you with data manipulation techniques such as *constraints*.

Relational tables and referential integrity have both been discussed several times in prior lessons. As I explained in those lessons, relational databases store data broken into multiple tables, each of which stores related data. Keys are used to create references from one table to another (thus the term *referential integrity*).

For relational database designs to work properly, you need a way to ensure that only valid data is inserted into tables. For example, if the Orders table stores order information and OrderItems stores order details, you want to ensure that any order IDs referenced in OrderItems exist in Orders. Similarly, any customers referred to in Orders must be in the Customers table.

Although you can perform checks before inserting new rows (do a SELECT on another table to make sure the values are valid and present), it is best to avoid this practice for the following reasons:

- ▶ If database integrity rules are enforced at the client level, every client is obliged to enforce those rules, and inevitably some clients won't.

- ▶ You must also enforce the rules on UPDATE and DELETE operations.

- ▶ Performing client-side checks is a time-consuming process. Having the DBMS do the checks for you is far more efficient.

NEW TERM: **Constraints**
Rules that govern how database data is inserted or manipulated.

DBMSs enforce referential integrity by imposing constraints on database tables. Most constraints are defined in table definitions (using CREATE TABLE or ALTER TABLE as discussed in Lesson 17, "Creating and Manipulating Tables").

> CAUTION: **Constraints Are DBMS Specific**
> There are several different types of constraints, and each DBMS provides its own level of support for them. Therefore, the examples shown here might not work as you see them. Refer to your DBMS documentation before proceeding.

Primary Keys

Lesson 1, "Understanding SQL," briefly discussed primary keys. A *primary key* is a special constraint used to ensure that values in a column (or set of columns) are unique and never change—in other words, a column (or columns) in a table whose values uniquely identify each row in the table. This facilitates the direct manipulation of and interaction with individual rows. Without primary keys, it would be difficult to safely use UPDATE or DELETE on specific rows without affecting any others.

Any column in a table can be established as the primary key, as long as it meets the following conditions:

▶ No two rows may have the same primary key value.

▶ Every row must have a primary key value. (Columns must not enable NULL values.)

▶ The column containing primary key values can never be modified or updated. (Most DBMSs won't enable this, but if yours does enable doing so, well, don't!)

▶ Primary key values can never be reused. If a row is deleted from the table, its primary key must not be assigned to any new rows.

One way to define primary keys is to create them as follows:

Input ▼

```
CREATE TABLE Vendors
(
    vend_id        CHAR(10)    NOT NULL PRIMARY KEY,
    vend_name      CHAR(50)    NOT NULL,
    vend_address   CHAR(50)    NULL,
    vend_city      CHAR(50)    NULL,
    vend_state     CHAR(5)     NULL,
    vend_zip       CHAR(10)    NULL,
    vend_country   CHAR(50)    NULL
);
```

Analysis ▼

In the above example, the keyword PRIMARY KEY is added to the table definition so that vend_id becomes the primary key.

Input ▼

```
ALTER TABLE Vendors
ADD CONSTRAINT PRIMARY KEY (vend_id);
```

Analysis ▼

Here the same column is defined as the primary key, but the CONSTRAINT syntax is used instead. This syntax can be used in CREATE TABLE and ALTER TABLE statements.

> NOTE: **Keys in SQLite**
> SQLite does not allow keys to be defined using ALTER TABLE and requires that they be defined as part of the initial CREATE TABLE.

Foreign Keys

A foreign key is a column in a table whose values must be listed in a primary key in another table. Foreign keys are an extremely important part of ensuring referential integrity. To understand foreign keys, let's look at an example.

The Orders table contains a single row for each order entered into the system. Customer information is stored in the Customers table. Orders in the Orders table are tied to specific rows in the Customers table by the customer ID. The customer ID is the primary key in the Customers table; each customer has a unique ID. The order number is the primary key in the Orders table; each order has a unique number.

The values in the customer ID column in the Orders table are not necessarily unique. If a customer has multiple orders, there will be multiple rows with the same customer ID (although each will have a different order number). At the same time, the only values that are valid within the customer ID column in Orders are the IDs of customers in the Customers table.

That's what a foreign key does. In our example, a foreign key is defined on the customer ID column in Orders so that the column can accept only values that are in the Customers table's primary key.

Here's one way to define this foreign key:

Input ▼

```
CREATE TABLE Orders
(
    order_num    INTEGER    NOT NULL PRIMARY KEY,
    order_date   DATETIME   NOT NULL,
    cust_id      CHAR(10)   NOT NULL REFERENCES Customers(cust_id)
);
```

Analysis ▼

Here the table definition uses the REFERENCES keyword to state that any values in cust_id must be in cust_id in the Customers table.

The same thing can be accomplished using CONSTRAINT syntax in an ALTER TABLE statement:

Input ▼

```
ALTER TABLE Orders
ADD CONSTRAINT
FOREIGN KEY (cust_id) REFERENCES Customers (cust_id);
```

> TIP: **Foreign Keys Can Help Prevent Accidental Deletion**
>
> As noted in Lesson 16, "Updating and Deleting Data," in addition to helping enforce referential integrity, foreign keys serve another invaluable purpose. After a foreign key is defined, your DBMS does not allow the deletion of rows that have related rows in other tables. For example, you are not allowed to delete a customer who has associated orders. The only way to delete that customer is to first delete the related orders (which in turn means deleting the related order items). Because they require such methodical deletion, foreign keys can help prevent the accidental deletion of data.
>
> However, some DBMSs support a feature called *cascading delete*. If enabled, this feature deletes all related data when a row is deleted from a table. For example, if cascading delete is enabled and a customer is deleted from the Customers table, any related order rows are deleted automatically.

Unique Constraints

Unique constraints are used to ensure that all data in a column (or set of columns) is unique. They are similar to primary keys, but there are some important distinctions:

▶ A table can contain multiple unique constraints, but only one primary key is allowed per table.

▶ Unique constraint columns can contain NULL values.

▶ Unique constraint columns can be modified or updated.

▶ Unique constraint column values can be reused.

▶ Unlike primary keys, unique constraints cannot be used to define foreign keys.

An example of the use of constraints is an Employees table. Every employee has a unique Social Security number, but you would not want to use it for the primary key because it is too long (in addition to the fact that you might not want that information easily available). Therefore, every employee also has a unique employee ID (a primary key) in addition to a Social Security number.

Because the employee ID is a primary key, you can be sure that it is unique. You also might want the DBMS to ensure that each Social Security number is unique too (to make sure that a typo does not result in the use of someone else's number). You can do this by defining a UNIQUE constraint on the Social Security number column.

The syntax for unique constraints is similar to that for other constraints. Either the UNIQUE keyword is defined in the table definition, or a separate CONSTRAINT is used.

Check Constraints

Check constraints are used to ensure that data in a column (or set of columns) meets a set of criteria that you specify. Common uses of this are

▶ **Checking minimum or maximum values**—For example, preventing an order of 0 (zero) items (even though 0 is a valid number)

▶ **Specifying ranges**—For example, making sure that a ship date is greater than or equal to today's date and not greater than a year from now

▶ **Allowing only specific values**—For example, allowing only M or F in a gender field

In other words, datatypes (discussed in Lesson 1) restrict the type of data that can be stored in a column. Check constraints place further restrictions within that datatype, and these can be invaluable in ensuring that the data that gets inserted into your database is exactly what you want. Rather than relying on client applications or users to get it right, the DBMS itself will reject anything that is invalid.

The following example applies a check constraint to the OrderItems table to ensure that all items have a quantity greater than 0:

Input ▼

```
CREATE TABLE OrderItems
(
    order_num     INTEGER     NOT NULL,
    order_item    INTEGER     NOT NULL,
    prod_id       CHAR(10)    NOT NULL,
    quantity      INTEGER     NOT NULL CHECK (quantity > 0),
    item_price    MONEY       NOT NULL
);
```

Analysis ▼

With this constraint in place, any row inserted (or updated) will be checked to ensure that quantity is greater than 0.

To check that a column named gender contains only M or F, you can do the following in an ALTER TABLE statement:

Input ▼

```
ADD CONSTRAINT CHECK (gender LIKE '[MF]');
```

> TIP: **User-Defined Datatypes**
> Some DBMSs enable you to define your own datatypes. These are essentially simple datatypes with check constraints (or other constraints) defined. For example, you can define your own datatype called gender that is a single-character text datatype with a check constraint that restricts its values to M or F (and perhaps NULL for Unknown). You could then use this datatype in table definitions. The advantage of custom datatypes is that the constraints need to be applied only once (in the datatype definition), and they are automatically applied each time the datatype is used. Check your DBMS documentation to determine if user-defined datatypes are supported.

Understanding Indexes

Indexes are used to sort data logically to improve the speed of searching and sorting operations. The best way to understand indexes is to envision the index at the back of a book (this book, for example).

Suppose you want to find all occurrences of the word *datatype* in this book. The simple way to do this would be to turn to page 1 and scan every line of every page looking for matches. Although that works, it is obviously not a workable solution.

Scanning a few pages of text might be feasible, but scanning an entire book in that manner is not. As the amount of text to be searched increases, so does the time it takes to pinpoint the desired data.

That is why books have indexes. An index is an alphabetical list of words with references to their locations in the book. To search for *datatype,* you find that word in the index to determine what pages it appears on. Then, you turn to those specific pages to find your matches.

What makes an index work? Simply, it is the fact that it is sorted correctly. The difficulty in finding words in a book is not the amount of content that must be searched; rather, it is the fact that the content is not sorted by word. If the content is sorted like a dictionary, an index is not needed (which is why dictionaries don't have indexes).

Database indexes work in much the same way. Primary key data is always sorted; that's just something the DBMS does for you. Retrieving specific rows by primary key, therefore, is always a fast and efficient operation.

Searching for values in other columns is usually not as efficient, however. For example, what if you want to retrieve all customers who live in a specific state? Because the table is not sorted by state, the DBMS must read every row in the table (starting at the very first row) looking for matches, just as you would have to do if you were trying to find words in a book without using an index.

The solution is to use an index. You may define an index on one or more columns so that the DBMS keeps a sorted list of the contents for its own use. After an index is defined, the DBMS uses it in much the same way as you would use a book index. It searches the sorted index to find the location of any matches and then retrieves those specific rows.

But before you rush off to create dozens of indexes, bear in mind the following:

▶ Indexes improve the performance of retrieval operations, but they degrade the performance of data insertion, modification, and deletion. When these operations are executed, the DBMS has to update the index dynamically.

▶ Index data can take up lots of storage space.

▶ Not all data is suitable for indexing. Data that is not sufficiently unique (State, for example) will not benefit as much from indexing as data that has more possible values (First Name or Last Name, for example).

▶ Indexes are used for data filtering and for data sorting. If you frequently sort data in a specific order, that data might be a candidate for indexing.

▶ Multiple columns can be defined in an index (for example, State plus City). Such an index will be of use only when data is sorted in State plus City order. (If you want to sort by City, this index would not be of any use.)

There is no hard-and-fast rule as to what should be indexed and when. Most DBMSs provide utilities you can use to determine the effectiveness of indexes, and you should use these regularly.

Indexes are created with the CREATE INDEX statement (which varies dramatically from one DBMS to another). The following statement creates a simple index on the Products table's product name column:

Input ▼

```
CREATE INDEX prod_name_ind
ON Products (prod_name);
```

Analysis ▼

Every index must be uniquely named. Here the name prod_name_ind is defined after the keywords CREATE INDEX. ON is used to specify the table being indexed, and the columns to include in the index (just one in this example) are specified in parentheses after the table name.

> TIP: **Revisiting Indexes**
> Index effectiveness changes as table data is added or changed. Many database administrators find that what once was an ideal set of indexes might not be so ideal after several months of data manipulation. It is always a good idea to revisit indexes on a regular basis to fine-tune them as needed.

Understanding Triggers

Triggers are special stored procedures that are executed automatically when specific database activity occurs. Triggers might be associated with INSERT, UPDATE, and DELETE operations (or any combination thereof) on specific tables.

Unlike stored procedures (which are simply stored SQL statements), triggers are tied to individual tables. A trigger associated with INSERT operations on the Orders table will be executed only when a row is inserted into the Orders table. Similarly, a trigger on INSERT and UPDATE operations on the Customers table will be executed only when those specific operations occur on that table.

Within triggers, your code has access to the following:

- ▶ All new data in INSERT operations

- ▶ All new data and old data in UPDATE operations

- ▶ Deleted data in DELETE operations

Depending on the DBMS being used, triggers can be executed before or after a specified operation is performed.

The following are some common uses for triggers:

- ▶ Ensuring data consistency; for example, converting all state names to uppercase during an INSERT or UPDATE operation

- ▶ Performing actions on other tables based on changes to a table; for example, writing an audit trail record to a log table each time a row is updated or deleted

- ▶ Performing additional validation and rolling back data if needed; for example, making sure a customer's available credit has not been exceeded and blocking the insertion if it has

- ▶ Calculating computed column values or updating time stamps

As you probably expect by now, trigger creation syntax varies dramatically from one DBMS to another. Check your documentation for more details.

The following example creates a trigger that converts the cust_state column in the Customers table to uppercase on all INSERT and UPDATE operations.

This is the SQL Server version:

Input ▼

```
CREATE TRIGGER customer_state
ON Customers
FOR INSERT, UPDATE
AS
UPDATE Customers
SET cust_state = Upper(cust_state)
WHERE Customers.cust_id = inserted.cust_id;
```

This is the Oracle and PostgreSQL version:

Input ▼

```
CREATE TRIGGER customer_state
AFTER INSERT OR UPDATE
FOR EACH ROW
BEGIN
UPDATE Customers
SET cust_state = Upper(cust_state)
WHERE Customers.cust_id = :OLD.cust_id
END;
```

> **TIP: Constraints Are Faster Than Triggers**
>
> As a rule, constraints are processed more quickly than triggers, so whenever possible, use constraints instead.

Database Security

There is nothing more valuable to an organization than its data, and data should always be protected from would-be thieves or casual browsers. Of course, at the same time data must be accessible to users who need access to it, and so most DBMSs provide administrators with mechanisms by which to grant or restrict access to data.

The foundation of any security system is user authorization and authentication. This is the process by which a user is validated to ensure he is who he says he is and that he is allowed to perform the operation he is trying to perform. Some DBMSs integrate with operating system security for this, others maintain their own user and password lists, and still others integrate with external directory services servers.

Here are some operations that are often secured:

▶ Access to database administration features (creating tables, altering or dropping existing tables, and so on)

▶ Access to specific databases or tables

▶ The type of access (read-only, access to specific columns, and so on)

▶ Access to tables via views or stored procedures only

▶ Creation of multiple levels of security, thus allowing varying degrees of access and control based on login

▶ Restrictions on the ability to manage user accounts

Security is managed via the SQL GRANT and REVOKE statements, although most DBMSs provide interactive administration utilities that use the GRANT and REVOKE statements internally.

Summary

In this lesson, you learned how to use some advanced SQL features. Constraints are an important part of enforcing referential integrity; indexes can improve data retrieval performance; triggers can be used to perform pre- or post-execution processing; and security options can be used to manage data access. Your own DBMS probably offers some form of these features. Refer to your DBMS documentation for more details.

APPENDIX A

Sample Table Scripts

Writing SQL statements requires a good understanding of the underlying database design. If you do not know what information is stored in what table, how tables are related to each other, and the actual breakup of data within a row, it is impossible to write effective SQL.

You are strongly advised to actually try every example in every lesson in this book. All the lessons use a common set of data files. To assist you in better understanding the examples, and to enable you to follow along with the lessons, this appendix describes the tables used, their relationships, and how to build (or obtain) them.

Understanding the Sample Tables

The tables used throughout this book are part of an order entry system used by an imaginary distributor of toys. The tables are used to perform several tasks:

▶ Manage vendors

▶ Manage product catalogs

▶ Manage customer lists

▶ Enter customer orders

Making this all work requires five tables (that are closely interconnected as part of a relational database design). A description of each of the tables appears in the following sections.

> NOTE: **Simplified Examples**
> The tables used here are by no means complete. A real-world order entry system would have to keep track of lots of other data that has not been included here (for example, payment and accounting information, shipment tracking, and more). However, these tables do demonstrate the kinds of data organization and relationships that you will encounter in most real installations. You can apply these techniques and technologies to your own databases.

Table Descriptions

What follows is a description of each of the five tables, along with the name of the columns within each table and their descriptions.

The `Vendors` Table

The `Vendors` table stores the vendors whose products are sold. Every vendor has a record in this table, and that vendor ID (the `vend_id`) column is used to match products with vendors.

TABLE A.1   `Vendors` Table Columns

Column	Description
vend_id	Unique vendor ID
vend_name	Vendor name
vend_address	Vendor address
vend_city	Vendor city
vend_state	Vendor state
vend_zip	Vendor ZIP code
vend_country	Vendor country

> ▶ All tables should have primary keys defined. This table should use `vend_id` as its primary key.

The `Products` Table

The `Products` table contains the product catalog, one product per row. Each product has a unique ID (the `prod_id` column) and is related to its vendor by `vend_id` (the vendor's unique ID).

TABLE A.2   `Products` Table Columns

Column	Description
prod_id	Unique product ID
vend_id	Product vendor ID (relates to `vend_id` in `Vendors` table)
prod_name	Product name
prod_price	Product price
prod_desc	Product description

▶ All tables should have primary keys defined. This table should use `prod_id` as its primary key.

▶ To enforce referential integrity, a foreign key should be defined on `vend_id` relating it to `vend_id` in VENDORS.

The `Customers` Table

The `Customers` table stores all customer information. Each customer has a unique ID (the `cust_id` column).

TABLE A.3 `Customers` Table Columns

Column	Description
cust_id	Unique customer ID
cust_name	Customer name
cust_address	Customer address
cust_city	Customer city
cust_state	Customer state
cust_zip	Customer ZIP code
cust_country	Customer country
cust_contact	Customer contact name
cust_email	Customer contact email address

▶ All tables should have primary keys defined. This table should use `cust_id` as its primary key.

The `Orders` Table

The `Orders` table stores customer orders (but not order details). Each order is uniquely numbered (the `order_num` column). Orders are associated with the appropriate customers by the `cust_id` column (which relates to the customer's unique ID in the `Customers` table).

TABLE A.4 `Orders` Table Columns

Column	Description
order_num	Unique order number
order_date	Order date
cust_id	Order customer ID (relates to cust_id in Customers table)

▶ All tables should have primary keys defined. This table should use order_num as its primary key.

▶ To enforce referential integrity, a foreign key should be defined on cust_id relating it to cust_id in CUSTOMERS.

The OrderItems Table

The OrderItems table stores the actual items in each order, one row per item per order. For every row in Orders there are one or more rows in OrderItems. Each order item is uniquely identified by the order number plus the order item (first item in order, second item in order, and so on). Order items are associated with their appropriate order by the order_num column (which relates to the order's unique ID in Orders). In addition, each order item contains the product ID of the item orders (which relates the item back to the Products table).

TABLE A.5   OrderItems Table Columns

Column	Description
order_num	Order number (relates to order_num in Orders table)
order_item	Order item number (sequential within an order)
prod_id	Product ID (relates to prod_id in Products table)
quantity	Item quantity
item_price	Item price

▶ All tables should have primary keys defined. This table should use order_num and order_item as its primary keys.

▶ To enforce referential integrity, foreign keys should be defined on order_num relating it to order_num in Orders and prod_id relating it to prod_id in Products.

Database administrators often use relationship diagrams to help demonstrate how database tables are connected. Remember, it is foreign keys that define those relationships as noted in the table descriptions above. Figure A.1 is the relationship diagram for the five tables described in this appendix.

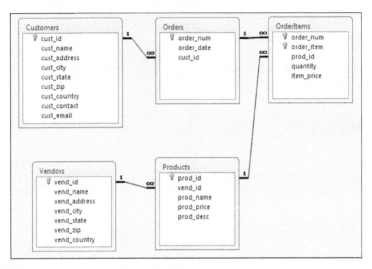

FIGURE A.1 Sample tables relationship diagram

Obtaining the Sample Tables

In order to follow along with the examples, you need a set of populated tables. Everything you need to get up and running can be found on this book's web page at `http://forta.com/books/0135182794/`.

On that page you'll find links to download SQL scripts for your DBMS. There are two files for each:

- `create.txt` contains the SQL statements to create the five database tables (including defining all primary keys and foreign key constraints).

- `populate.txt` contains the SQL INSERT statements used to populate these tables.

The SQL statements in these files are very DBMS specific, so be sure to execute the one for your own DBMS. These scripts are provided as a convenience to readers, and no liability is assumed for problems that may arise from their use.

At the time that this book went to press, scripts were available for

- IBM DB2 (including Db2 on Cloud)

- Microsoft SQL Server (including Microsoft SQL Server Express)

- MariaDB

- ▶ MySQL

- ▶ Oracle (include Oracle Express)

- ▶ PostgreSQL

- ▶ SQLite

TIP: **SQLite Data File**

SQLite stores its data in a single file. You can use the creation and population scripts to create your own SQLite data file. Or, to make things easier, you can download a ready-to-use file from the URL above.

Other DBMSs may be added as needed or requested.

NOTE: **Create, Then Populate**

You must run the table creation scripts *before* the table population scripts. Be sure to check for any error messages returned by these scripts. If the creation scripts fail, you will need to remedy whatever problem may exist before continuing with table population.

NOTE: **Specific DBMS Setup Instructions**

The specific steps used to set up your DBMS vary greatly based on the DBMS used. When you download the scripts or databases from the book's web page, you'll find a README file that provides specific setup and installation steps for specific DBMSs.

SQL Statement Syntax

To help you find the syntax you need when you need it, this appendix lists the syntax for the most frequently used SQL operations. Each statement starts with a brief description and then displays the appropriate syntax. For added convenience, you'll also find cross-references to the lessons where specific statements are taught.

When reading statement syntax, remember the following:

▶ The | symbol is used to indicate one of several options, so NULL|NOT NULL means specify either NULL or NOT NULL.

▶ Keywords or clauses contained within square brackets [like this] are optional.

▶ The syntax listed below will work with almost all DBMSs. You are advised to consult your own DBMS documentation for details of implementing specific syntactical changes.

ALTER TABLE

ALTER TABLE is used to update the schema of an existing table. To create a new table, use CREATE TABLE. See Lesson 17, "Creating and Manipulating Tables," for more information.

Input ▼

```
ALTER TABLE tablename
(
  ADD|DROP  column  datatype  [NULL|NOT NULL]  [CONSTRAINTS],
  ADD|DROP  column  datatype  [NULL|NOT NULL]  [CONSTRAINTS],
  ...
);
```

COMMIT

COMMIT is used to write a transaction to the database. See Lesson 20, "Managing Transaction Processing," for more information.

Input ▼

```
COMMIT [TRANSACTION];
```

CREATE INDEX

CREATE INDEX is used to create an index on one or more columns. See Lesson 22, "Understanding Advanced SQL Features," for more information.

Input ▼

```
CREATE INDEX indexname
ON tablename (column, ...);
```

CREATE PROCEDURE

CREATE PROCEDURE is used to create a stored procedure. See Lesson 19, "Working with Stored Procedures," for more information. Oracle uses a different syntax as described in that lesson.

Input ▼

```
CREATE PROCEDURE procedurename [parameters] [options]
AS
SQL statement;
```

CREATE TABLE

CREATE TABLE is used to create new database tables. To update the schema of an existing table, use ALTER TABLE. See Lesson 17 for more information.

Input ▼

```
CREATE TABLE tablename
(
    column    datatype    [NULL|NOT NULL]    [CONSTRAINTS],
    column    datatype    [NULL|NOT NULL]    [CONSTRAINTS],
    ...
);
```

CREATE VIEW

CREATE VIEW is used to create a new view of one or more tables. See Lesson 18, "Using Views," for more information.

Input ▼

```
CREATE VIEW viewname AS
SELECT columns, ...
FROM tables, ...
[WHERE ...]
[GROUP BY ...]
[HAVING ...];
```

DELETE

DELETE deletes one or more rows from a table. See Lesson 16, "Updating and Deleting Data," for more information.

Input ▼

```
DELETE FROM tablename
[WHERE ...];
```

DROP

DROP permanently removes database objects (tables, views, indexes, and so forth). See Lessons 17 and 18 for more information.

Input ▼

```
DROP INDEX|PROCEDURE|TABLE|VIEW indexname|procedurename|tablename|
viewname;
```

INSERT

INSERT adds a single row to a table. See Lesson 15, "Inserting Data," for more information.

Input ▼

```
INSERT INTO tablename [(columns, ...)]
VALUES(values, ...);
```

INSERT SELECT

INSERT SELECT inserts the results of a SELECT into a table. See Lesson 15 for more information.

Input ▼

```
INSERT INTO tablename [(columns, ...)]
SELECT columns, ... FROM tablename, ...
[WHERE ...];
```

ROLLBACK

ROLLBACK is used to undo a transaction block. See Lesson 20 for more information.

Input ▼

```
ROLLBACK [TO savepointname];
```

or

Input ▼

```
ROLLBACK TRANSACTION;
```

SELECT

SELECT is used to retrieve data from one or more tables (or views). See Lesson 2, "Retrieving Data," Lesson 3, "Sorting Retrieved Data," and Lesson 4, "Filtering Data," for more basic information. (Lessons 2–14 cover aspects of SELECT.)

Input ▼

```
SELECT columnname, ...
FROM tablename, ...
[WHERE ...]
[UNION ...]
[GROUP BY ...]
[HAVING ...]
[ORDER BY ...];
```

UPDATE

UPDATE updates one or more rows in a table. See Lesson 16 for more information.

Input ▼

```
UPDATE tablename
SET columnname = value, ...
[WHERE ...];
```

APPENDIX C

Using SQL Datatypes

As explained in Lesson 1, "Understanding SQL," datatypes are essentially rules that define what data may be stored in a column and how that data is actually stored.

Datatypes are used for several reasons:

- ▶ Datatypes enable you to restrict the type of data that can be stored in a column. For example, a numeric datatype column will only accept numeric values.

- ▶ Datatypes allow for more efficient storage, internally. Numbers and date-time values can be stored in a more condensed format than text strings.

- ▶ Datatypes allow for alternate sorting orders. If everything is treated as strings, 1 comes before 10, which comes before 2. (Strings are sorted in dictionary sequence, one character at a time starting from the left.) As numeric datatypes, the numbers would be sorted correctly.

When designing tables, pay careful attention to the datatypes being used. Using the wrong datatype can seriously impact your application. Changing the datatypes of existing populated columns is not a trivial task. (In addition, doing so can result in data loss.)

Although this appendix is by no means a complete tutorial on datatypes and how they are to be used, it explains the major datatype types, what they are used for, and compatibility issues that you should be aware of.

> CAUTION: **No Two DBMSs Are Exactly Alike**
>
> It's been said before, but it needs to be said again. Unfortunately, datatypes can vary dramatically from one DBMS to the next. Even the same datatype name can mean different things to different DBMSs. Be sure you consult your DBMS documentation for details on exactly what it supports and how.

String Datatypes

The most commonly used datatypes are string datatypes. These store strings: for example, names, addresses, phone numbers, and ZIP codes. There are basically two types of string datatypes that you can use—fixed-length strings and variable-length strings (see Table C.1).

Fixed-length strings are datatypes that are defined to accept a fixed number of characters, and that number is specified when the table is created. For example, you might allow 30 characters in a first-name column or 11 characters in a Social-Security-number column (the exact number needed allowing for the two dashes). Fixed-length columns do not allow more than the specified number of characters. They also allocate storage space for as many characters as specified. So, if the string Ben is stored in a 30-character first-name field, a full 30 characters are stored (and the text may be padded with spaces as needed).

Variable-length strings store text of any length (the maximum varies by datatype and DBMS). Some variable-length datatypes have a fixed-length minimum. Others are entirely variable. Either way, only the data specified is saved (and no extra data is stored).

If variable-length datatypes are so flexible, why would you ever want to used fixed-length datatypes? The answer is performance. DBMSs can sort and manipulate fixed-length columns far more quickly than they can sort variable-length columns. In addition, many DBMSs will not allow you to index variable-length columns (or the variable portion of a column). This also dramatically impacts performance. (See Lesson 22, "Understanding Advanced SQL Features," for more information on indexes.)

TABLE C.1 String Datatypes

Datatype	Description
CHAR	Fixed-length string from 1 to 255 characters long. Its size must be specified at create time.
NCHAR	Special form of CHAR designed to support multibyte or Unicode characters. (The exact specifications vary dramatically from one implementation to the next.)
NVARCHAR	Special form of TEXT designed to support multibyte or Unicode characters. (Exact specifications vary dramatically from one implementation to the next.)
TEXT (also called LONG or MEMO or VARCHAR)	Variable-length text.

Numeric Datatypes

Numeric datatypes store numbers. Most DBMSs support multiple numeric datatypes, each with a different range of numbers that can be stored in it. Obviously, the larger the supported range, the more storage space needed. In addition, some numeric datatypes support the use of decimal points (and fractional numbers), whereas others support only whole numbers. Table C.2 lists common uses for various datatypes, but not all DBMSs follow the exact naming conventions and descriptions listed here.

TABLE C.2 Numeric Datatypes

Datatype	Description
BIT	Single-bit value, either 0 or 1, used primarily for on/off flags
DECIMAL (also called NUMERIC)	Fixed or floating-point values with varying levels of precision
FLOAT (also called NUMBER)	Floating-point values
INT (also called INTEGER)	4-byte integer value that supports numbers from −2147483648 to 2147483647
REAL	4-byte floating-point values
SMALLINT	2-byte integer value that supports numbers from −32768 to 32767
TINYINT	1-byte integer value that supports numbers from 0 to 255

> TIP: **Not Using Quotes**
> Unlike strings, numeric values should never be enclosed within quotes.

> TIP: **Currency Datatypes**
> Most DBMSs support a special numeric datatype for storing monetary values. Usually called MONEY or CURRENCY, these datatypes are essentially DECIMAL datatypes with specific ranges that make them well suited for storing currency values.

Date and Time Datatypes

All DBMSs support datatypes designed for the storage of date and time values (see Table C.3). Like numeric values, most DBMSs support multiple datatypes, each with different ranges and levels of precision.

TABLE C.3   Date and Time Datatypes

Datatype	Description
DATE	Date value
DATETIME (also known as TIMESTAMP)	Date-time values
SMALLDATETIME	Date-time values with accuracy to the minute (no seconds or milliseconds)
TIME	Time value

> CAUTION: **Specifying Dates**
> There is no standard way to define a date that will be understood by every DBMS. Most implementations understand formats like 2020-12-30 or Dec 30th, 2020, but even those can be problematic to some DBMSs. Make sure to consult your DBMS documentation for a list of the date formats that it will recognize.

> TIP: **ODBC Dates**
> Because every DBMS has its own format for specifying dates, ODBC created a format of its own that will work with every database when ODBC is being used. The ODBC format looks like {d '2020-12-30'} for dates, {t '21:46:29'} for times, and {ts '2020-12-30 21:46:29'} for date-time values. If you are using SQL via ODBC, be sure your dates and times are formatted in this fashion.

Binary Datatypes

Binary datatypes are some of the least compatible (and, fortunately, also some of the least used) datatypes. Unlike all the datatypes explained thus far, which have very specific uses, binary datatypes can contain any data, even binary information, such as graphic images, multimedia, and word processor documents (see Table C.4).

TABLE C.4 Binary Datatypes

Datatype	Description
BINARY	Fixed-length binary data (maximum length may vary from 255 bytes to 8,000 bytes, depending on implementation)
LONG RAW	Variable-length binary data up to 2GB
RAW (called BINARY by some implementations)	Fixed-length binary data up to 255 bytes
VARBINARY	Variable-length binary data (maximum length varying from 255 bytes to 8,000 bytes is typical, depending on implementation)

> **NOTE: Comparing Datatypes**
>
> If you would like to see a real-world example of database comparisons, look at the table creation scripts used to build the example tables in this book (see Appendix A, "Sample Table Scripts"). By comparing the scripts used for different DBMSs, you'll see firsthand just how complex a task datatype matching is.

APPENDIX D
SQL Reserved Words

SQL is a language made up of keywords—special words that are used in performing SQL operations. Special care must be taken to not use these keywords when naming databases, tables, columns, and any other database objects. Thus, these keywords are considered reserved.

This appendix contains a list of the more common reserved words found in major DBMSs. Please note the following:

▶ Keywords tend to be very DBMS-specific, and not all the keywords that follow are used by all DBMSs.

▶ Many DBMSs have extended the list of SQL reserved words to include terms specific to their implementations. Most DBMS-specific keywords are not listed in the following list.

▶ To ensure future compatibility and portability, it is a good idea to avoid any and all reserved words, even those not reserved by your own DBMS.

ABORT	ARE	BEFORE
ABSOLUTE	AS	BEGIN
ACTION	ASC	BETWEEN
ACTIVE	ASCENDING	BIGINT
ADD	ASSERTION	BINARY
AFTER	AT	BIT
ALL	AUTHORIZATION	BLOB
ALLOCATE	AUTO	BOOLEAN
ALTER	AUTO-INCREMENT	BOTH
ANALYZE	AUTOINC	BREAK
AND	AVG	BROWSE
ANY	BACKUP	BULK

BY	CONFIRM	DBCC
BYTES	CONNECT	DEALLOCATE
CACHE	CONNECTION	DEBUG
CALL	CONSTRAINT	DEC
CASCADE	CONSTRAINTS	DECIMAL
CASCADED	CONTAINING	DECLARE
CASE	CONTAINS	DEFAULT
CAST	CONTAINSTABLE	DELETE
CATALOG	CONTINUE	DENY
CHANGE	CONTROLROW	DESC
CHAR	CONVERT	DESCENDING
CHARACTER	COPY	DESCRIBE
CHARACTER_LENGTH	COUNT	DISCONNECT
CHECK	CREATE	DISK
CHECKPOINT	CROSS	DISTINCT
CLOSE	CSTRING	DISTRIBUTED
CLUSTER	CUBE	DIV
CLUSTERED	CURRENT	DO
COALESCE	CURRENT_DATE	DOMAIN
COLLATE	CURRENT_TIME	DOUBLE
COLUMN	CURRENT_TIMESTAMP	DROP
COLUMNS	CURRENT_USER	DUMMY
COMMENT	CURSOR	DUMP
COMMIT	DATABASE	ELSE
COMMITTED	DATABASES	ELSEIF
COMPUTE	DATE	ENCLOSED
COMPUTED	DATETIME	END
CONDITIONAL	DAY	ERRLVL

ERROREXIT	FROM	INTERVAL
ESCAPE	FULL	INTO
ESCAPED	FUNCTION	IS
EXCEPT	GENERATOR	ISOLATION
EXCEPTION	GET	JOIN
EXEC	GLOBAL	KEY
EXECUTE	GO	KILL
EXISTS	GOTO	LANGUAGE
EXIT	GRANT	LAST
EXPLAIN	GROUP	LEADING
EXTEND	HAVING	LEFT
EXTERNAL	HOLDLOCK	LENGTH
EXTRACT	HOUR	LEVEL
FALSE	IDENTITY	LIKE
FETCH	IF	LIMIT
FIELD	IN	LINENO
FIELDS	INACTIVE	LINES
FILE	INDEX	LISTEN
FILLFACTOR	INDICATOR	LOAD
FILTER	INFILE	LOCAL
FLOAT	INNER	LOCK
FLOPPY	INOUT	LOGFILE
FOR	INPUT	LONG
FORCE	INSENSITIVE	LOWER
FOREIGN	INSERT	MANUAL
FOUND	INT	MATCH
FREETEXT	INTEGER	MAX
FREETEXTTABLE	INTERSECT	MERGE

MESSAGE	OPEN	PROCESSEXIT
MIN	OPTION	PROTECTED
MINUTE	OR	PUBLIC
MIRROREXIT	ORDER	PURGE
MODULE	OUTER	RAISERROR
MONEY	OUTPUT	READ
MONTH	OVER	READTEXT
MOVE	OVERFLOW	REAL
NAMES	OVERLAPS	REFERENCES
NATIONAL	PAD	REGEXP
NATURAL	PAGE	RELATIVE
NCHAR	PAGES	RENAME
NEXT	PARAMETER	REPEAT
NEW	PARTIAL	REPLACE
NO	PASSWORD	REPLICATION
NOCHECK	PERCENT	REQUIRE
NONCLUSTERED	PERM	RESERV
NONE	PERMANENT	RESERVING
NOT	PIPE	RESET
NULL	PLAN	RESTORE
NULLIF	POSITION	RESTRICT
NUMERIC	PRECISION	RETAIN
OF	PREPARE	RETURN
OFF	PRIMARY	RETURNS
OFFSET	PRINT	REVOKE
OFFSETS	PRIOR	RIGHT
ON	PRIVILEGES	ROLLBACK
ONCE	PROC	ROLLUP
ONLY	PROCEDURE	ROWCOUNT

RULE	STARTING	UNTIL
SAVE	STARTS	UPDATE
SAVEPOINT	STATISTICS	UPDATETEXT
SCHEMA	SUBSTRING	UPPER
SECOND	SUM	USAGE
SECTION	SUSPEND	USE
SEGMENT	TABLE	USER
SELECT	TABLES	USING
SENSITIVE	TEMP	VALUE
SEPARATOR	TEMPORARY	VALUES
SEQUENCE	TEXT	VARCHAR
SESSION_USER	TEXTSIZE	VARIABLE
SET	THEN	VARYING
SETUSER	TIME	VERBOSE
SHADOW	TIMESTAMP	VIEW
SHARED	TO	VOLUME
SHOW	TOP	WAIT
SHUTDOWN	TRAILING	WAITFOR
SINGULAR	TRAN	WHEN
SIZE	TRANSACTION	WHERE
SMALLINT	TRANSLATE	WHILE
SNAPSHOT	TRIGGER	WITH
SOME	TRIM	WORK
SORT	TRUE	WRITE
SPACE	TRUNCATE	WRITETEXT
SQL	TYPE	XOR
SQLCODE	UNCOMMITTED	YEAR
SQLERROR	UNION	ZONE
STABILITY	UNIQUE	

Index

To...	See...

Frequently Used SQL Statements

ALTER TABLE

ALTER TABLE is used to update the schema of an existing table.
To create a new table use CREATE TABLE.
See Lesson 17, "Creating and Manipulating Tables."

COMMIT

COMMIT is used to write a transaction to the database.
See Lesson 20, "Managing Transaction Processing."

CREATE INDEX

CREATE INDEX is used to create an index on one or more columns.
See Lesson 22, "Understanding Advanced SQL Features."

CREATE TABLE

CREATE TABLE is used to create new database tables.
To update the schema of an existing table use ALTER TABLE.
See Lesson 17, "Creating and Manipulating Tables."

CREATE VIEW

CREATE VIEW is used to create a new view of one or more tables.
See Lesson 18, "Using Views."

DELETE

DELETE deletes one or more rows from a table.
See Lesson 16, "Updating and Deleting Data."

DROP

DROP permanently removes database objects (tables, views, indexes, and so on).
See Lesson 17, "Creating and Manipulating Tables," and Lesson 18, "Using Views."

INSERT

INSERT adds a single row to a table.
See Lesson 15, "Inserting Data."

INSERT SELECT

INSERT SELECT inserts the results of a SELECT into a table.
See Lesson 15, "Inserting Data."

ROLLBACK

ROLLBACK is used to undo a transaction block.
See Lesson 20, "Managing Transaction Processing."

SELECT

SELECT is used to retrieve data from one or more tables (or views).
See Lesson 2, "Retrieving Data," Lesson 3, "Sorting Retrieved Data," and Lesson 4, "Filtering Data." (Lessons 2 through 14 all cover various aspects of SELECT).

UPDATE

UPDATE updates one or more rows in a table.
See Lesson 16, "Updating and Deleting Data."